The World of Toni Morrison
Explorations in Literary Criticism

Bessie W. Jones
Audrey L. Vinson
Alabama A. & M. University

COLLEGE FOR HUMAN SERVICES
LIBRARY
345 HUDSON STREET
NEW YORK, N.Y. 10014

Kendall/Hunt Publishing Company
Dubuque, Iowa

This edition has been printed directly from the authors' manuscript copy.

Copyright © 1985 by Kendall/Hunt Publishing Company

ISBN 0-8403-3763-9

All rights reserved. No part of this publication may be reproduced, stored in a retrieval system, or transmitted, in any form or by any means, electronic, mechanical, photocopying, recording, or otherwise, without the prior written permission of the copyright owner.

Printed in the United States of America

B   403763   01

In Honor of Our Mothers

and

In Memory of Our Fathers

FOREWORD

Toni Morrison's four novels — *The Bluest Eye, Sula, Song of Solomon* and *Tar Baby* have made a great impact on American readers. Morrison's voice, though a recent one in American fiction, is mature and profound. From the outset with the publication of *The Bluest Eye* (1970), her genius was apparent. Her subjects and themes are familiar, but her approaches to them are distinctly different from any other American author.

Morrison's themes, settings, motifs, symbols, characters, and style offer a great challenge to the critic. It is the purpose of these essays to examine Morrison's canon from these critical perspectives. We have attempted to be inclusive in our treatment of the novels, but we make no claim of having been exhaustive in our approaches to the study of the novels. Also included in this volume is an interview with Toni Morrison in her office at Random House which we think gives a great deal of insight into Morrison's perceptivity.

We express sincere appreciation to our families for their encouragement, patience, and perseverance during the preparation of these essays.

Bessie W. Jones
Audrey L. Vinson

Alabama A. and M. University
Huntsville, Alabama

TONI MORRISON

Martha Kaplan

CHRONOLOGY

1931 Toni Morrison born Chloe Anthony Wofford on February 18, in Lorain, Ohio.

1949 Graduated with honors from the Lorain Public Schools.

1953 Graduated from Howard University, Washington, D.C.

1955 Received master's degree in English from Cornell University.

1955 Began teaching career at Texas Southern University in Houston, Texas.

1957 Became instructor of English at Howard University where she taught until 1964.

1964 Became associate editor with L. W. Singer Publishing Company, a subsidiary of Random House.

1967 Transferred to Random House as a senior editor.

1970 *The Bluest Eye* published.

1974 *Sula* published.

1977 *Song of Solomon* published.

   Received the National Book Critics Circle Award for Fiction

1981 *Tar Baby* published.

TABLE OF CONTENTS

FOREWORD   v

CHRONOLOGY   vii

INTRODUCTION   1
    Audrey L. Vinson

1. The Other World of Toni Morrison   7
    Audrey L. Vinson

2. Ironic Use of Fairy Tale Motifs in   25
The Bluest Eye
    Bessie W. Jones

3. Vacant Places: Setting in the Novels   37
of Toni Morrison
    Audrey L. Vinson

4. Psychological Disorientation in *Sula*   49
    Bessie W. Jones

5. Pilate Dead: Conjuress   63
    Audrey L. Vinson

6. Pilate Dead: A Symbol of the   81
Creative Imagination
    Bessie W. Jones

7. Anarchy in *Song of Solomon*   89
    Audrey L. Vinson

8. Greek Tragic Motifs in *Song of Solomon*   103
    Bessie W. Jones

9. Garden Metaphor and Christian   115
Symbolism in *Tar Baby*
    Bessie W. Jones

10. An Interview with Toni Morrison   127
    Bessie W. Jones

BIBLIOGRAPHY   155

INDEX   157

Introduction

No single approach could reveal the range and depth of Toni Morrison's novels, for her plots, characters, themes and literary devices are diverse and evocative of numerous modes of analysis which one book cannot exhaust. This multiplicity contains an overwhelming number of components which interact to give us a dazzling prism which her total work becomes. It is, therefore, difficult to find a word or phrase that would fairly identify or define the canon. Although any attempt at encapsulating the works is fraught with the risks of incompletion, one inevitably arrives at an umbrella phrase which covers at least a great part of the art of Toni Morrison. Her works are metaphors of escape which visually and aurally transport characters out of the confines of reality into freeing ideals.

These metaphors are revealed in numerous ways which are both traditional and innovative, for as a writer Miss Morrison encompasses many modes of expression. An important way is through imagery. *The Bluest Eye*, a novel about a young girl, Pecola, who wishes that her eyes were blue so that she will fit what she sees as the norm of beauty which is superimposed on her milieu, revolves around a dominant image of blue eyes. Pecola is seen through the eyes of Claudia, another child who is the novel's narrator. The experiences of black children growing up amid the standards of the larger, white society are conveyed through a number of images which are both grotesque and ordinary. Blue eyes seem to stare from the background in surrealistic dominance as references to the characters in a first grade reader, Dick and Jane, present the ideal lives which contrast sharply with the starkness in the environment of the black children. Blue eyes are in Pecola's unfulfilled dream and hence are ever before the reader throughout the novel, and the tangible Shirley Temple doll with which the girls play has blue eyes. Furthermore, the little daughter of the employer of Pecola's mother has blue eyes. The image remains, in some way, like a painfully blinding light, an instrument of torture throughout the novel. The longing is intensified when Pecola is driven further into escapism after being sexually assaulted by her father. Thus, the plot moves towards its pathetic end through the actions of innocent children who must learn to look beyond themselves for fulfillment. In her combined works, Morrison's imagery ranges from simple nature to the exotic and spectacular. Birds in *The Bluest Eye*, *Sula* and *Song of Solomon* are significant images serving at times as totem figures. Magical costume and color add to the visual richness, while the sounds of nature, the street and the black idiom combine with other sensations to produce a rich blend of images which contribute in important ways to the development of the plots.

A second metaphor of escape in Morrison's work is in the form of the supernatural. Sula, the third generation of "manloving" women, is given in the novel *Sula*, supernatural qualities which remove her from the ordinary people of Medallion. She breaks out of the bonds of her small town, lives in various cities for a number of years, and returns with an innate resistance to the accepted norms of life in Medallion. When she returns, birds die, forewarning the residents that bad times are ahead. The unnatural power which she exerts results in nearly everyone succumbing to it, even the husband of her best friend, Nel. Sula and Nel grew up in Medallion with little else except their mutual trust. Nel conformed to the life in her town and lived relatively untroubled until her husband was seduced by Sula. While other characters are different, even grotesque in some ways, Sula, her mother, Hannah, and her grandmother, Eva Peace, represent a fatal dynasty which is nourished by some inherent need to escape reality by exploiting it. Supernatural elements are significantly utilized in Morrison's other novels. In *Song of Solomon* the flying African, Pilate's navelless abdomen, her conjuring, and apparitions pervade the novel and are components of the vehicles by which characters flee their circumstances and take flight toward self-discovery. Equally fantastic elements appear in *Tar Baby* in Son's superhuman swim, his control over other characters, the wild horsemen, and Mary Therese's perpetual flow of milk.

A third form of the metaphor of escape is in rhetorical devices such as point of view, syllogistic thought, negations and ambivalence. *Song of Solomon*, a novel which relates Milkman Dead's search for his identity, reveals the mechanism by which his aunt and guide, Pilate Dead, leads him to their ancestral home. Milkman's life is traced from the day he was born at Mercy Hospital, a memorable day because a man killed himself in a spectacular jump from the roof of the white, segregated hospital which Milkman's pregnant mother happened to be near. His birth integrated the hospital. Although he is the son of the town's most prosperous black man, Milkman's childhood is marred by his father's greed and the strange personality of his mother who nursed him for nearly half his childhood. With Pilate's help, he travels a circuitous road in a long search which is punctuated by an alliance with, then severance from, his cousin and lover, Hagar, and his friend, Guitar; encounters with a group whose sole aim is to avenge deaths of blacks and which called itself the Seven Days; his meeting with Circe; and finally, the attainment of the missing clue to his identity in the children's song which contained the key to the mystery of the Flying African, his great grandfather. Through multiple points of view, Morrison conveys Milkman's escape to find himself by requiring the combined viewpoints of Pilate, Ruth Dead, Macon Dead, and Circe. A different kind of rhetorical device is the extended rationale of the Seven Days in *Song of Solomon*. Logical thought derived from premises and conclusions gives Guitar his equation for anarchy.

Negations are used in *Song of Solomon* to circumvent the naming of things by the white power structure. Hence, the segregated Mercy Hospital becomes, to the black community, No Mercy Hospital; the strange, white child in *Sula* was named Tarbaby; the

Bottom (the black section of the town of Medallion) was actually a mountain. Also in *Sula*, the shocking terror of Chicken Little's drowning is a form of negation since Sula and Nel passively watched him drown without attempting a rescue.

Ambivalences in the form of transformations, conversions and pairing of characters abound in Morrison's work. Pilate's ubiquity in *Song of Solomon* enabled her to transform herself into more than one person at a given time. In a similar way, Circe was at once dainty and filthy, and though very old, had the voice of a twenty-year old girl. Soaphead *(The Bluest Eye)* "had a hatred of, and fascination with any hint of disorder or decay." Like him, Shadrack *(Sula)* possessed many aberrant, uneven traits, but kept a neat cottage. These ambivalences underscore the psychological and physical duality of the isolated black community.

In *Tar Baby*, a successful, smartly dressed and educated young black model in Paris catches a glimpse of a beautiful African woman in a Parisian market. Jadine, the model, looks at the woman in yellow, whose skin is like tar, with awe - "Just a quick snatch of breath before that woman's woman- that mother/ sister/ she; that unphotographable beauty - took it all away. [The woman] turned those eyes too beautiful for eyelashes on Jadine and, with a small parting of her lips, shot an arrow of saliva between her teeth down to the pavement..." (46).* Despite the woman's rejection of her, Jadine experiences a sudden self-revelatory longing for her inward self while she just as suddenly perceives her Paris experience as a "show." She cables her aunt and uncle in Dominique who are cook and butler to Valerian Street, and she is off to the Caribbean leaving behind a sparkling career and offers of marriage. She has left the show.

---

*From TAR BABY, by Toni Morrison. Copyright (c) 1981 by Toni Morrison. Reprinted by permission of Alfred A. Knopf, Inc.

Thus begins Jadine's quest for identity, spurred by her meeting with a kind of Ur-Blackness in the African woman. She had been made to feel unauthentic by the woman in yellow. Her quest, therefore, would have to yield authenticity. The journey can be traced through the paradigm of the heroic quest in myth and her guide is Son, the unaffected, authentic conjuror who wields power, magic, and pleasure with equal abandon among the occupants of the Street villa. His total lack of pretension attracts Jadine, for she unconsciously longs to remove the mask she has worn for years as she participated in the "show." Jadine's quest is typical of a fourth form of the metaphor of escape in the Morrison canon - ritual. In *Tar Baby* there is further abundant ritual in the form of Son's rite of rebirth, his power and incantations. In the other novels, many instances of ritual involve transformations, homeopathy, spiritism, the uncanny and visions. There are, of course, the many instances of ritual born of the street culture depicted in the novels.

The ideals to which Morrison's characters attempt to escape are the archetypal paradises of physical habitat and the more abstract apotheosis of atonement and self-discovery. Miss Morrison is equally adept in treating both kinds. Attempts to emerge from such depths as the psychological chasms of Pecola, Shadrack or Son, the metaphoric cosmic hell of the Sein de Veilles, the terrifying swamp in *Tar Baby*, or the depths of Pilate's wine house from Milkman emerged, trace the struggles of Morrison's characters to failure or dubious success. Jadine could not remain in the depths, while Son had always lived in Hell and felt at home there (in his instinctive habit of living). But it was disconcerting to Jadine to be so starkly exposed to her instincts. Hence, she sought the escape which led her back to Paris.

Finally, the suffering of Morrison's characters and its resulting knowledge deserve examination from the standpoint of Greek tragedy, for Morrison, like the tragedians, makes significant statements about morality, virtue and justice. Her characters are often critics who are judging evil and giving meaning to the absurd in their lives. Soaphead, like Pentheus, defies God, while Eva Peace *(Sula)* exerts an irrational, Euripidean fury against herself and her child. Echoes of the lyrical beauty and dignity of Aeschylus and Sophocles can be found in Milkman's elevation and Son's hubris and resulting exile.

This brief outline of a number of Morrison's literary devices is not intended to suggest that they will all be treated in the essays which are in this book. While several of them are treated, these broad references are mentioned here to suggest the variety of technique in her work. In addition, the essays which follow are independent of each other. Yet, they often reflect the same elements of Morrison's style from different stances. Moreover, the essays provide detailed substantiation of the metaphor of escape which the novels reflect. Toni Morrison's canon, which consists of four novels, is artistically distinctive. She leaves her readers with much to anticipate in future works.

1
THE OTHER WORLD OF TONI MORRISON

Despite the recency of Toni Morrison's emergence as a significant American writer, her work reflects the grotesque as an American genre in the tradition of writers which include Sherwood Anderson, Richard Wright, Andrew Lytle, Flannery O'Conner, Eudora Welty and William Faulkner. The appeal of the grotesque is authenticated by the similarities in images and figuration utilized by these fiction writers. Such physical abnormalities as lameness in Faulkner and O'Connor, the locked bowels of Mrs. Ritter's child in *The Velvet Horn* by Andrew Lytle and the locked bowels of Eva Peace's son, Plum, are examples of a unanimity in grotesque imagery which abounds in much American fiction. The images function as symbols of extreme circumstances dealt by nature or society and the human responses to them. This use of the grotesque is meta-realism, if I may suggest a term, a combination of realism and fabulistic image which magnifies a social dilemma. Morrison, as with others in the tradition of the grotesque, moves beyond reality to symbols which enable us to focus with unusual clarity on an aspect of American life. Abnormalities, absurdities and bizarre circumstances emerge in the tradition of meta-realism to link these writers in a way that transcends region and ethnicity and reaches the core of the American experience as characters are confronted by problems of both hope and despair.

The novels of Toni Morrison depict black persons whose enveloping world heaps upon them a conglomeration of ideals, images and experiences which the reality of their lives belies. Characters are forced into creative improvisations which are responses to their non-conventional experiences. These improvisations are often bizarre actions which free certain individuals to cope with their "other world." We are introduced to this other world through several devices of the grotesque which include absurd incongruities, the arabesque, and a Dantean conception of death. Either directly or implicitly counterparts in the white world provide the norms by which aberrant actions are measured. Morrison's characters, although Midwestern and Eastern, can be placed in any town in America - any town with its black side of town. Hence, it is an isolated place where the necessary dual consciousness becomes one of the burdens of life. By the standards of the engulfing society, i.e., white society, the place is nowhere. But Morrison demonstrates that her characters are creative artists "making up" life from day to day. Thus we have the other world of Toni Morrison, a world presented through a dominating set of grotesqueries. Fanciful or fantastic representations lift her characters out of normal ranges and validate the "tests" which they undergo in proving who they are. These grotesqueries may be categorized according to several types which are prominently depicted and they can be shown to contribute to the thematic purpose of the author.

The first set of grotesqueries can be categorized as physical abnormalities. In *The Bluest Eye* Pecola's Mother, Pauline, had a foot which "saved" her from complete anonymity. At two years of age a nail punched through her foot and left it "Crooked, archless and flopping" when she walked. Morrison infers that, except for the abnormality, Pauline would never have left the confines of a world which had largely ignored her. Her daughter Pecola, also ignored, inflicts a self-imposed abnormality on herself when she persists in her desire to have blue eyes. The former wishing, grotesque enough, becomes an achieved fact to Pecola, who never regains contact with reality. Soaphead, the conjuror, has usurped God's creation by altering Pecola's eyes. Thereafter, her life is lived through this supposed acquisition of a physical feature which would cause her to be universally and spontaneously loved by all who saw her. The "blue eyes" promote Morrison's purpose of revealing the absurdity of maintaining unrealistic standards which are narrowly defined and are applicable to only one group of people.

Maureen Peal, the "high yellow dream child" in *The Bluest Eye*, represents the grotesque since her white skin contrasts sharply with the complexion of other black children. Especially grotesque is the comic absurdity of the reaction of the darker skinned children to her. This is true particularly in Pecola's exaggerated admiration of Maureen, whose hair was "braided into two lynch ropes." Morrison's superimposition, in chapter headings, of Dick and Jane, characters in a first grade reader, unites with the Maureen Peal image to emphasize the psychological burden of the black child as she copes with a domineering caucasian image of physical beauty which fosters self-hatred. Maureen's function in the plot is in the way her color alienates her, a smaller version of the heroine of Ernest Gaines' *Catherine Carmier* in which the isolation of Catherine from other blacks is inherent in the social structure. Maureen enhances the theme of the novel through the absurdity of society's demand that one must be white and she promotes feelings of inferiority in the darker children who are constantly bombarded by this standard.

Physical abnormalities are employed in *Sula* to underscore futility and the absurdity of existence. Sula's physical perfection (except for a small birthmark on her face) was her abnormality: she had no childhood diseases and she was invulnerable to gnats or mosquitoes. Morrison's purpose in devising this odd circumstance apparently has to do with her inference that Sula is supernatural and a conjure woman. Hence, her power over the lives of other people is much more credible with such a portrayal than it would be if she were an average person who falls prey to measles and chicken pox. Also in *Sula* is the gruesome history of Eva Peace's leg, allegedly lost through deliberately placing it on the railroad track for the purpose of collecting money from the insurance company. Again the futility of a poverty stricken life has provided the impetus for this act which is a part of Morrison's characters "creating life" as they go. They are originals who improvise solutions stemming from themselves and not from the larger society. Consequently, there is no "traditional" or "accepted" mode of problem solving in *Sula*. While Sula's grotesque qualities are natural, Eva's severed leg is selfwilled. They both illustrate the novel's thematic purpose in showing the conflict between nature and society and the extremes to which that conflict impels characters to "design" their own lives.

Physical abnormalities in *Song of Solomon* often repeat the functions identified in *The Bluest Eye* and *Sula*. By the time Miss Morrison writes her third novel, however, she exercises more subtlety and complexity in her handling of these images. Milkman's left leg is shorter than the right leg. He discovers this himself at fourteen.

> When he stood barefoot and straight as a pole, his left foot was about half an inch off the floor. So he never stood straight; he slouched or leaned or stood with a hip thrown out and he never told anybody about it - ever. When Lena said, "Mama what is he walking like <u>that</u> for?" he said, "I'll walk any way I want to including over your ugly face." ...It wasn't a limp - not at all - just the strut of a very young man trying to appear more sophisticated than he was.   (62)*

Milkman even relates his deformity to President Roosevelt and feels secretly related to him. This slight physical variance erects a protective fence around Milkman which is visible only to him. While others interpret his limp as affectation, he uses his abnormality to create his own image of himself without outside interference. This does not mean, however, that Milkman does not suffer the typical adolescent exaggeration of an imperfection - agonizing over what he considered a "burning" defect. But he recreates life with others by exploiting it, as his unique dancing became an object of fascination which the

---

*From SONG OF SOLOMON, by Toni Morrison. Copyright(c)1977 by Toni Morrison. Reprinted by permission of Alfred A. Knopf, Inc.

girls loved and which other boys copied. Hence, Milkman becomes an example of coping with an abnormality which is useful in the later thematic development of Pilate who must also cope with an unusual physical circumstance.

The character Pilate, Milkman's aunt, possesses one startling feature, a smooth abdomen with no navel. This sets her apart from ordinary people, embues her with mystery and makes her the object of ridicule and fear. Her grotesque quality is enhanced by the wearing of one earring, a pendant basket containing her name on a slip of paper. Pilate is one of Morrison's most enigmatic characters. Like Sula she has the status of a conjure woman - supernatural and powerful. All major characters in the novel eventually gravitate to Pilate who holds the key to their lives and while navelless, is the matrix of the plot. Ruth Dead, representing the opposite pole in social standing, breaks years of deliberate alienation to visit Pilate. Milkman frequents her home, first out of curiosity and defiance, and later, to see Hagar. In addition, much of the motivation for Guitar's actions is in Pilate's supposed wealth. The symbolic richness of Pilate as a character cannot be overlooked. She is the fundamental link with Milkman's past. From her amulets and memory, as well as from her instinctive regard for primal values regarding her family, she is a character deserving extensive analysis. The multiplicity of grotesque qualities surrounding her converge to convey the major events in the novel.

The grotesque exhibited in the life of First Corinthians, Milkman's sister, stems from the absurdity and unnatural aspect of a young woman working as a maid after she has finished Bryn Mawr and traveled in Europe. She is included in the category of physical abnormalities because she posed as a professional woman, even to the extent of leaving home each morning dressed for a professional job. Upon arrival at her place of work, however, she would put on her maid's uniform, "drop to her knees" and scrub the floor. Corinthians' employer, upon seeing her unusual ability, eventually allowed her to type. This physical transformation of herself into a professional type gives meaning to Corinthian's life. She creates her image in the face of the denials inherent in her segregated environment. In this respect, she faces the dilemma of isolation imposed by society. Her improvisation serves Morrison's intention of depicting the burden of racial isolation.

In *Tar Baby*, the African woman in Paris has eyes too beautiful for eyelashes. Therese, the island washwoman who is a former nursemaid, has nursed at her breasts many white babies, and she still has milk in her breasts many years later. These abnormalities symbolize in the African woman the primal sights of those eyes which had "burnt away their lashes" (47). In Therese, the breasts with their perpetual flow of milk identify her as mother of the island and they reinforce the portrayal of her as nourisher and guide. This extension of the grotesque is a possible continuation of the archetypal images of nourisher and guide already portrayed in the characters Pilate and Circe.

Toni Morrison employs commemorative days in *Sula*, *Song of Solomon* and *Tar Baby* as reflections of the grotesque. In *Sula* National Suicide Day is celebrated by the shell shocked war veteran Shadrack. Upon his return from the war, he is the sole celebrant as he parades down the streets of the Bottom. Eventually he is joined by the grotesque characters, Tar Baby and the deweys. This seemingly absurd activity becomes the conveyor of the climatic action of the novel as the whole town, sane and otherwise, join the parade for what indeed turns out to be a suicide march. An unusual commemorative in *Song of Solomon* was the day when Mercy Hospital admitted blacks. It was the day of Robert Smith's jump and the patient was Ruth Dead, going into labor as she witnessed Smith's jump. This day is referred to often enough in the novel to mark it as a special commemorative which has meaning for nearly everyone in Milkman's milieu. In *Tar Baby* Margaret Street's sterile attempts to create a normal Christmas celebration on the island only magnifies the guilt and suffering from abusing her child whose

Christmas visit she hopes will result in atonement. Various social problems elicit these commemoratives: war, segregation and child abuse. Through these commemoratives, Morrison expands her interest in extreme circumstances dealt by society.

Names often reflect the grotesque in Morrison's work. In *The Bluest Eye,* Soaphead Church, the man who "saves" Pecola by probably hypnotizing her and having her believe that her eyes have become blue, derives the first part of his name from the arabesque quality of the "tight, curly hair that took on a sheen and wave when pomaded with soap lather. A sort of primitive process" (132).* Soaphead's legitimate name was Elihue Micah Whitcomb. "Church" was added to his name by virtue of his having studied theology and his having been known at the time of his arrival in Medallion as a guest preacher. "All in all his personality was arabesque: Intricate, symmetrical, balanced, and tightly constructed - except for one flaw. The careful design was marred occasionally by rare but keen sexual cravings" (132). Yet Morrison has Soaphead's aberrations coalescing with those of Pecola and other "lost souls" and he becomes the medium who solves their problems. The novel resolves its own theme with absurd problems evoking absurd solutions.

In her next novel, Sula, Morrison increases the absurd references through the medium of names. A long list of characters from this novel have names which are highly ironic or mythic. Several such names follow:

(1) Eva Peace, whose violent life left no room for peace.

(2) Shadrack, the ironic opposite of the captive in the third chapter of Daniel, for the Biblical Shadrack came out of the blazing

---

*From THE BLUEST EYE by Toni Morrison. Copyright(c)1970 by Toni Morrison. Reprinted by permission of Holt, Rinehart, Winston.

furnace unharmed. If the war which left Morrison's character shell-shocked is the analogue of the furnace, then Morrison possibly infers that Shadrack is sane and logical in his celebration of National Suicide Day.

(3) Ajax, the street macho who eventually cohabits with Sula, is thought at first by Sula to be A. Jacks. The mythical Ajax, a swift, capable warrior, serves as a parallel to the adept Ajax in *Sula*.

(4) The deweys - three homeless boys who are never thought of as individuals and who consequently think and act in unison. (Closely related in purpose is the use of "Mary" and "Yardman" as names for servants in *Tar Baby*. All female island servants were "Mary" and Gideon, the yardman, was never called Gideon by the occupants of the mansion.

(5) Tar Baby (formerly Pretty Johnny) who is described by Morrison as another homeless boy with milky skin and cornsilk hair. As with the deweys, Tar Baby simply appeared.

Some names in *Song of Solomon* are definite Biblical references: Pilate, First Corinthians, and Magdalena. Morrison's enigmatic Pilate has enormous power which is ironically comparable to the power wielded by Pontius Pilate. More likely than this relationship, however, is the sheer ludicrousness of the name for a girl or woman. With Magdalena, called Lena, there is the obvious contrast between the fallen, sinful Magdalene of the Bible and the selfless and moral character created by Morrison. In *Tar Baby*, Therese (also called Mary) takes Son to the far side of the isle to run with the wild horsemen, the original inhabitants of the isle. Hence she enforces a rebirth in harmony with her name Mary and his name -

Son. These names contribute much to the overall grotesque effect which pervades the novels.

Like names, commercial objects often evoke the absurd and ludicrous. The Shirley Temple doll in *The Bluest Eye* represents the great beauty to which Pecola aspires. Nu-Nile Hair Oil and Mary Janes are other examples of images which are symbolic of existing standards of beauty or their attainment. In *Song of Solomon* Hagar's Joyce shoes are her tokens of the ultimate in being chic. As utilized by Morrison, these objects are not valued in and for themselves, but for the elevation of human hopes which they generate. They are, therefore, symbols of illusive ideals. Furthermore, they reflect the popular culture of the time. Yet the popular values held by the white, dominant society are useless, ridiculous and often humorous when applied to blacks. Popular culture in Morrison becomes highly stratified by implication. Even within practically the same geographical area, the popular concepts of whites do not logically apply to the submerged black culture. Hence Morrison's characters further substantiate their need to improvise, to create their own lives.

This ability to create in some characters does not prevent the extreme psychological dilemmas which lead to insanity. Thus insanity is a form of the grotesque in all four novels. Morrison's "insane" characters often have painfully authentic insights. In *The Bluest Eye*, Pecola's unreasonable wish to have blue eyes is a capitulation to the demands of an unfair society which acknowledges only caucasian beauty. In the same novel, Soaphead's irrational behavior is his intellectual response to the absurdity of life. His understanding of the emotionally distraught and his strongly rhetorical letter to God reflect the reason and thought which he has given the dilemma of human hopelessness. In *Song of Solomon* Hagar's insanity is pure animism. When Milkman breaks away from her, she is wildly angry and without restraint, striking against that which would separate her from her strongest desire. Robert Smith's insanity is the overwhelming effect of his membership in the Seven Days, a murderous society whose sole purpose is to avenge black lives taken by whites. Smith has obviously "snapped" after carrying out numerous acts which are counter to his actual moral beliefs. Within the same organization, Guitar's obsession with his "mission" leaves him a dangerous, irrational man who sees only too clearly the only means of hope left to a trapped people. In *Sula* Shadrack's rantings contained truth after all, and it is ironic that no one at first shared his insight or even respected it. The war experience opened his mind to the reality and ugliness of life, but he could not convey this truth without being ridiculed. His "enlightenment", therefore, was a lonely retreat from the dark ignorance of ordinary people. Another form of mental aberration in *Sula* is Eva Peace, Sula's grandmother. She is an example of Morrison's characters who improvise and create their own lives. The dilemma of a son (Plum), too dependent on her and drugs, and increasingly making attempts to return to her womb, caused her to douse him with gasoline and burn him alive. Her violent solutions to problems did not exclude harm to herself. According to Sula, when Eva had no means of caring for her family, she placed her leg on the railroad track to be cut off. The resulting settlement with the insurance company improved her circumstance. The crazed Therese in *Tar Baby* knows that unbridled passion is preventing Son from becoming a whole person. Hence she delivers him to the place he deserves to go, to the untamed side of the island. These irrational responses to insolvable problems contribute to the grotesque character of Morrison's novels. They reflect with brilliance her thematic approach to contradictions in society which have no apparent logical solutions.

Still another category of the grotesque is in plagues and natural devastation. In *The Bluest Eye*, the flower seeds, superstitiously planted by two young girls to help give life to Pecola's unborn child, never grew. The novel opens with the following lines:

> Quiet as it's kept, there were no marigolds in the fall of 1941. We thought it was because Pecola was

> having her father's baby that the marigolds did not grow.
> A little examination and much less melancholy would have
> proved to us that our seeds were not the only ones that
> did not sprout; nobody's did. Not even the gardens
> fronting the lake showed marigolds that year.   (1)

Morrison has the narrator (Claudia) conclude that rather than being the fault of any person, the sterile gardens were the result of the unyielding earth. This use of the grotesque carries the inference that Pecola and others are victims of powerful forces over which nothing prevails.

In *Sula* a plague of robins accompanied Sula's return to the Bottom after a long absence. The symbolic significance of the plague is obviously Sula's own devastating path which she cuts across the Bottom.

> The little yam-breasted shuddering birds were every-
> where ...At Eva's house there were four dead robins on
> the walk. Sula stopped and with her toe pushed them into
> the bordering grass ...When Sula opened the door (Eva)
> raised her eyes and said, "I might have knowed them birds
> meant something. Where's your coat?   (91)*

Of course, everyone in the Bottom knew the birds meant the arrival of evil days. "What was taken by outsiders to be slackness, slovenliness or even generosity was in fact a full recognition of the legitimacy of forces other than good ones" (90). Yet the plague, with its accompanying evil, is not as startling as the event at the bridge site. As Shadrack leads his National Suicide Day paraders across the embankment, the earth gives in and buries many people alive. These persons were the jobless and the unwanted. Again, a "solution" has been created, this time by nature. The devastation is at once an evil and a

---

*From SULA, by Toni Morrison. Copyright (c) 1973 by Toni Morrison. Reprinted by permission of Alfred A. Knopf, Inc.

benevolence. Morrison implies, furthermore, that the marchers instinctively joined the parade as a final act of protest against an unkept promise.

Perhaps the ultimate grotesquerie in Morrison's work is death with a Dantean justice. Prominent in the novels is the irresistible attraction, or magnetism, of death. Even when there is a desperate hanging onto life, the strongly expressed wish for death is implicit. In *Sula* the characters have a lifestyle that flirts with death. Death becomes the problem solver; hence, Chicken Little, Plum, Hannah and Sula die according to an equation which is inevitable. In *Song of Solomon*, given the circumstances of the dangerous hunt on behalf of the Seven Days, death is an inexorable force which must be accepted, occasionally dealt, and as with Milkman, made a part of the momentary expectation of existence.

In Dante's *Divine Comedy* punishment in the Inferno is meted out inversely according to and in proportion to the sin. Justice in Toni Morrison's cosmos is similarly dealt. This is especially true in *Sula*. Hannah, who loved red tomatoes, while aflame and running, had a pot of tomatoes (which were being prepared for canning) thrown on her in a futile attempt to save her life. As an extended symbol, the tomatoes further symbolize Hannah's knowledge of the carnage committed by her mother which Hannah has passively accepted.

The most vivid meting of Dantean justice is seen in the earth slide at the site of the proposed bridge, a project which was a promise of jobs to the desperately poor people of the Bottom. Mrs. Jackson, who loved to eat ice "...weighing less than 100 pounds, slid down the bank and met with an open mouth the ice she had craved all her life" (162). Morrison utilizes Dantean justice in *Tar Baby* to emphasize the willful ignoring of reason in Son. His desire to live by instinct and passion condemns him forever to the punishment of running wild to the thundering hooves of the horsemen on the Isle des Chevaliers. The tableaux created through the imagery of Hannah's tomatoes, Mrs. Jackson's ice, and Son's perpetual running, in their shocking evocation of justice prevailing even among persons who have already suffered, are drawn superbly. As tableaux, they remain with the reader for a long time, compelling one to think about the social dilemmas which they symbolize.

These grotesqueries are startling, and whether they are physical, commemorative or reflective of justice, they are tableaux making dramatic statements about plot and theme. As elements in the novels, they represent the concretizing of social statements and are important stylistic devices in Toni Morrison's work. Explicit images shine brilliantly through the novels as graphic representations of personal and social dilemmas. The results are paintings which speak with depth about the problems of characters. Morrison stated in her interview with Bessie Jones that painting, rather than literature, influenced her most in determining imagery in her work. Through scenes described in vivid language Morrison was able to create tableaux that render meaning to theme. These tableaux are compositions or groupings which express the main elements of specific themes. Like the frozen figures on Keats' urn, they externalize ideas as both action and stasis. They include theme supporting images which are totemic and imagery of pageantry, alienation, justice and the supernatural. As bizarre hybrid composites, they function dynamically in eliciting from the reader fresh thoughts on issues which are otherwise rhetorically well worn. While this technique has been used with good results before in novels, Morrison's tableaux, with their grotesque elements, strike the reader as dramatic statement. It is the effect that one finds in drama which is evoked by her tableaux.

While Morrison's social statement is different, it is useful to refer to a form of tableaux introduced by Bertolt Brecht in his epic theatre. His idea of educating the proletariat to the necessity of changing their lives was implemented through a form which he called *gestus*. Gestic elements are like tableaux in being graphic representations and summations of attitudes, and they contain social statements which Brecht felt was the greatest responsibility of the playwright. He often revised scenes so that they reflected social purpose and relevancy. While Brecht put the elements of his tableaux in simple, familiar frames, Morrison is often surrealistic and complex. They differ, too, in Brecht's obviously Marxist sentiment and Morrison's more specific apprehension of motive in her black characters. Yet, her tableaux can be seen through the gestic modes of deprivation, alienation and atonement.

Through colorful, often grotesque, scenes Morrison was able to create tableaux that render meaning to her themes. A common characteristic of these tableaux is their composition as groupings of the main agents of exploitation, deprivation, alienation and other themes treated by her. In *The Bluest Eye* the tableaux revolve around the contrasts evident in two juxtaposed worlds - white and black. The drab house of Claudia and Frieda is superimposed on the ideal house in the storybook. The "picture" is a collage in which need is superimposed on plenty. It thus appears starker and uglier than if it were seen in isolation. The dark, roach-ridden environment of Pecola and her friends is magnified by the brightness of the house in which Dick and Jane live. When Morrison provides close-ups of this environment, we discover that human beings, like houses, are superimposed in collage-like fashion. The tableau of the two little black girls caressing with motherly concern a blue-eyed white doll and enrapt with its beauty is a graphic statement of the ludicrousness of applying white standards of beauty to blacks. The reality of blacks caring for white children is not the intended meaning of the tableau, but the acceptance of white standards while rejecting black qualities is the intent. The social statement made in the tableau calls attention to the origin of self-hatred in many black children. The ultimate collage is the projected idea of Pecola possessing blue eyes exactly like those of Shirley Temple. The "wrongness" of the combination is less shocking than its eeriness. The same eeriness is evoked when Pecola's mother, in a similarly grouped tableau, is shown preferring the white child of her employer to her own child. The hatred and disdain felt toward Pecola is counterbalanced with love and care for the white child. The reader is forced to review the psychological and social import of this tableau.

The device of the grotesque in character and plot becomes, in Morrison's work, an inverted glass which reflects a gallery containing often shocking tableaux. The characters' actions are inverted toward themselves in a strongly existential manner. I feel justified in using the term existential, for Morrison herself explains in *Sula* that Sula's was "an experimental life" and "...she had no center, no speck around which to grow...she was completely free of ambition...no ego" (119). William Faulkner created characters with no egos, but their distortion is not as pervasive as the categories cited above. Yet one must ask why Morrison's characters turn inward upon themselves with such distortion. With one possible exception her characters persist in actions which result in self immolation in various forms. Jadine, in *Tar Baby*, inwardly "kills" her *self* in returning to Paris where she will play roles. The one attempt at a projected action for change is Guitar in *Song of Solomon*. In his work with the Seven Days, he is anarchistic, but he has a social consciousness missing in other characters. Yet Morrison's characters, with all their aberrations, are freer than conventional ones which fit into the accepted molds of society. They are experimenters whose lives conduct us through the most intimately dark and terrifying passages of our psyches.

QUESTIONS

1. Read a short story or a novel by one of the authors referred to at the beginning of this essay and compare or contrast the use of the grotesque images with that of Toni Morrison.

2. Indicate whether Morrison's use of absurd elements reduces or heightens your identification with certain characters.

3. Show how surrealism in fiction is comparable to surrealistic painting (or any other art form).

4. List and give the significance of characters' names which are not mentioned in this essay.

5. Commercial objects have long stood for standards to which some people aspire. If Morrison's novels were set in 1985, what objects would serve her purpose in this regard?

6. Apply, as a layman, some aspect of psychological criticism to one of the characters mentioned in that portion of the essay which deals with insanity.

7. Read the first canto of Dante's Divine Comedy. Show other ways in which Morrison's characters experience Dantean justice.

8. In one or more of Morrison's novels, reconstruct several tableaux which make social statements. Select those not mentioned in the essay.

2 IRONIC USE OF FAIRY TALE MOTIFS IN THE BLUEST EYE

Toni Morrison's *The Bluest Eye* abounds in fairy tale motifs that result in a plot and characters that are bitterly ironic and shockingly realistic. Such fairy tale motifs as wish-fulfillment, magic and enchantment, witches, and ill-treated child, the abusive step-parent, color imagery, and the fairy godmother are among the features that are woven into the woof and warp of *The Bluest Eye*, a novel which is a very dark and bitter depiction of the life of a young black girl growing up in white America in the early 1940's.

It is very obvious as the novel begins that Morrison wishes to suggest a child-like view of the world in her opening paragraph which is patterned after the familiar primers used in the first grade by many children beginning school in the 1930's and 40's.

> Here is the house. It is green and white. It has a red door. It is very pretty. Here is the family. Mother, Father, Dick and Jane live in the green and white house. They are very happy. See Jane. She has a red dress. She wants to play. Who will play with Jane? See the Cat. It goes meow-meow. Come and play. Come and play with Jane. The kitten will not play. See Mother. Mother is very nice. Mother, will you play with Jane? Mother laughs. Laugh, Mother, laugh. See Father. He is big and strong. Father, will you play with Jane? Father is smiling. Smile, Father, smile. See the dog. Bow-wow goes the dog. Do you want to play with Jane? See the dog run. Run, dog, run. Look, look. Here comes a friend. The friend will play with Jane. They will play a good game. Play, Jane, play.   (1)

Portions of this paragraph are used contrastively at the beginning of each section of the novel. Supposedly, this is the picture of the ideal American family which is held up as a model not only in the schools, but also in magazine advertisements, in the picture shows and on billboards.

But this world of fairy tale or storybook enchantment is immediately juxtaposed with the world of stark reality which Claudia, the nine-year old narrator, describes.

> Our house is old, cold and green. At night a kerosene lamp lights one large room. The others braced in darkness, peopled by roaches and mice. Adults do not talk to us - they give us directions. They issue orders without providing information. When we trip and fall down they glance at us; if we cut or bruise ourselves, they ask us are we crazy. When we catch colds, they shake their heads in disgust at our lack of consideration. How, they ask us, do you expect anybody to get anything done if you are sick? We cannot answer them. Our illness is treated with contempt, foul Black Draught, and castor oil that blunts our minds. (5-6)

The sharp contrast between the placid and peaceful surroundings of Dick and Jane and the environment in which Claudia lives underscores one aspect of the irony of *The Bluest Eye*. Here life is no fairy tale; there is no happy ending. Here the day to day struggle for survival is sometimes a nightmare. Where Dick and Jane enjoy life, Claudia and her ten-year old sister Frieda simply endure it. Where Mother and Father have time to play with Dick and Jane, Mother and Father do not even have time to talk to Claudia and Frieda. Where the kitten and the dog are the standard playmates of Dick and Jane, Claudia is more concerned about the roaches and mice that move among the darkness in their home. There is little joy and laughter surrounding Claudia and Frieda, only adult disgust and contempt.

In depicting this contrastive view of life, Morrison underscores the dilemma with which the black child had to deal-- the make-believe world of which he had no part and the real world with which he was all too familiar. He was brainwashed in the schools to believe that what he read and saw was what he had to approximate. Morrison repeatedly underscores the irony of this situation.

By relating the story from the point of view of a child, a technique familiar to fairy tale lore, Morrison's bitter satire and brutal realism are subtlely revealed. Although many young children are highly impressionable, Claudia, the young narrator is more highly perceptive than most children her age. In fact, the reader forgets that the narrator is a child, for indeed Claudia has the wisdom and insight of many far older than she. Together she and her sister Frieda, her alter-ego, see life through the eyes of experience though their story is shrouded in the guise of the innocence of childhood.

"Here comes a friend. The friend will play with Jane. They will play a good game. Play, Jane, play" (1). And a "friend" does come to play with Claudia and Frieda; only she is a "case" to whom Claudia and Frieda must be kind. The game they play is not a "good" game. It is the game of initiation and survival.

Pecola Breedlove, the "case" who comes to live with Claudia and Frieda temporarily, is the main character of the novel. She is the composite of many fairy-tale heroines, except she is no heroine. She is an ironical caricature of the fairy-tale heroine. She is a victim of the absurdities of the society that envelops her. She is the ugly duckling, but, unfortunately, she does not change into a swan. She is the abused and ill-treated step-child, but the abusive step-parents are ironically her own mother and father. The mirror into which she stares does not reassure her that she is the "fairest of them all." Her entire existence is blurred by her self-image of her ugliness perpetuated by what she reads and sees. "Long hours she sat looking in the mirror trying to discover the secret of the ugliness, the ugliness that made her ignored or despised at school by teachers and classmates alike" (34). Pecola's low self-esteem is reiterated in her admiration of Maureen Peal, a "high-yellow dream child" whose "summery complexion" and sloe-green eyes sharply contrast with Pecola's blackness. The absurdities reflected in the subtle allusions to the fairy tale lore of the ugly duckling, Cinderella and Snow White are exceeded only by the absurdities that Pecola faced in real life.

Pecola attributed all of the abusiveness that she received from her classmates, her teachers, her parents and others who were unkind to her to the fact that she was black and ugly. Even those persons who were as black as she, contemptuous of their own blackness, taunted Pecola with cries of "Black e mo. Black e mo..." (50). At this point, Morrison underscores the tragedy of the self-hatred and racial negativism reflected in the attitude of blacks toward themselves. The insult becomes more injurious when the same remarks are chanted by the half-white Maureen Peal.

Pecola's father and mother, Cholly and Pauline Breedlove, epitomize the mean step-parents of fairy tale lore, but ironically they are her natural parents. It is expected in fairy-tale lore that the father should marry a selfish second wife who mistreats the child and vice versa, but it is ironical when the natural parents and step-parents exchange roles. All of her life Pecola endured the violence imposed upon her by natural parents. Both Cholly and Mrs. Breedlove, as Pecola called her mother, were mean to each other as well as to Pecola and her brother Sammy. Cholly, mean *and* ugly, was so shiftless and contrary that in a fit of rage he burned the family dwelling down and left himself and family "outdoors," the most disgraceful thing that could happen to humankind. Moreover, Mrs. Breedlove thrived on her own "holiness" and Cholly's diabolism.

Cholly Breedlove represents that breed of black males caught in the lower depths who vented their anger and frustration against society and their own plight with the violence they perpetrated on their families. Often bitter because of demeaning work or no work at all, blighted hopes and thwarted dreams, they resigned themselves to the physical and mental emasculation imposed upon them by white America and exerted their "manhood" through physical prowess at home and in the black community. The tragedy of Cholly's plight is that nobody ever asked "why?" "The why is always difficult." No matter how serious his malfeasance, Cholly was always put in the workhouse. Whether he needed psychiatric care or medical care or both, he was simply sent to the country workhouse. Finally, he died there.

The ironical role that Mrs. Breedlove performs as "nanny" to the daughter of her white mistress and the meanness that she displays with her own daughter, Pecola, is typical of the play-acting that many black maids engaged in for survival. Most often to the neglect of their own families they cared for the house and families of the white mistress. They simulated love for the children of the mistress as in the scene involving Mrs. Breedlove and her mistress' "little pink and yellow daughter." Pecola accidentally pulled a blueberry pie from the table painfully burning her own leg. Mrs. Breedlove's anger toward Pecola was expressed irately: "'Crazy fool...my floor, mess... look what you....work....get on out....now that.... crazy....my floor, my floor: Her words were hotter and darker than the smoking berries...'" (84-85).

In response to the startled cries of her mistress' little pink and white girl Mrs. Breedlove consoled with "'Hush, baby hush. Come here. Oh Lord, look at your dress. Don't cry no more. Polly will change it'" (85). The irony of this situation reaches its climax in the fact that the mistress' little girl refers to Pauline Breedlove as "Polly" while her own daughter Pecola, calls her "Mrs. Breedlove."

In fairy-tale lore often the names of the characters are allegorical. But Cholly Breedlove's surname is the antithesis of what he represents. Throughout the novel Morrison reiterates the strong desire that Pecola has to be loved. Pecola even felt that, "If she looked different, beautiful, maybe Cholly would be different, and Mrs. Breedlove too. Maybe they'd say, "Why, look at pretty-eyed Pecola. We mustn't do bad things in front of those pretty eyes" (34). But in the Breedlove household, what was bred was hatred, not love. The most bitingly satirical example of the hatred bred by Cholly Breedlove is in his violating the body of his own twelve year-old daughter, Pecola, and impregnating her. All of the fiendishness of his being is epitomized in this diabolical act. Here the fairy-tale ironically becomes a monster and horror tale and Cholly's Satanic nature is epitomized.

Even Pecola's pregnancy and Cholly's confinement in the workhouse did not cause Mrs. Breedlove's meanness and abusiveness towards her daughter to diminish. Whenever the violence and abusiveness became too much to endure for her brother, he ran away from home. But where physical flight was his means of escape from the reality of his degrading life, Pecola engaged in mental flight. She fantasized. She longed for the blue eyes that she felt would cause all her trials and frustration to evaporate. She had even seen these glass blue eyes on the face of a black cat who was loved and coddled by Miss Geraldine, Junior's mother. Both Sammy's and Pecola's actions reflect methods of escape that many blacks of the period participated in. Leaving points South and moving North many blacks found the physical flight was futile because similar problems often awaited the escapees in less obvious ways. Mental flight often led to psychological impairment as in the case of Pecola who never regained contact with reality after her eyes were "changed."

The Bluest Eye is not without the witches common to fairy-tale lore. That role is fulfilled by three ladies of the evening-- "three merry gargoyles," "three merry harridans" named Miss Marie, called the Maginot Line, China and Poland. These three immediately elicit images of the three Furies of Greek mythology and the three witches of Shakespeare's "Macbeth." These three "fantastics" live in the apartment above the Breedlove's storefront. It is ironical that everyone else in town (except their clients) avoid them like the plague, but Pecola adores them. They belong to her world of fantasy. Their little favors in the form of ice cream and candy money for Pecola endear them to her. The trinkets that they wear, their cheap perfume and highly painted faces are masks that they wear to help them escape the ugliness of their existence.

Claudia and Frieda were terrified when they learned that Pecola knew these three "bad" women, especially the Maginot Line. She was the one who had killed people, poisoned them, boiled them in dye and even set them on fire. Church women "would not let their eyes rest on her," and Mrs. MacTeer, Claudia and Frieda's mother, said she "wouldn't let her eat out of one of her plates." Of the Maginot Line Pecola says, "Miss Marie is nice. They all nice" (82). Pecola even fantasized about their "niceness." She said: "They give me stuff all the time...Oh lots of stuff, pretty dresses and shoes. I got more shoes than I can ever wear. And jewelry and candy and money. They take me to the movies, and once we went to the carnival. China gone take me to Chicago to see the Loop. We going everywhere together" (83). It is not strange that Pecola would admire Miss Marie especially because Miss Marie called her all of those loving names that no one else called her-- "Dumplin'," "Puddin'" and "Chittlin'" -- names "chosen from menus and dishes that were forever uppermost in Marie's mind" (38). Being around these fancy women afforded Pecola the opportunity to indulge in her own fantasies just as these three lived in a world of fantasy. Their constant stream of laughter, the songs they sang about being blue "'cause I', sleeping' by myself" and "I know a boy who is sky-soft brown," and their ability to wear the world as a loose garment caused Pecola to look and look at them and wonder if they were real. Their talk about love was especially appealing to Pecola for whom love was an elusive dream. She was deeply concerned about how to get someone to love her and a part of her desire to get new eyes was to elicit love first from Cholly and Mrs. Breedlove and then from the others who she thought despised her.

These witches --Miss Marie, China and Poland-- fulfill a role in Pecola's life far from what is the usual conception of the witch in a fairy-tale lore. They are "good" witches so far as Pecola is concerned regardless of how "bad" the majority of the community feels that they are. Their celluloid and cellophane world is comparable to Pecola's image of beauty. They offer her one form of escape.

Color imagery so typical of fairy tale lore abounds in *The Bluest Eye*. Youthfulness, jollity, vibrancy and innocence are reflected in Morrison's blending of "streaks of green from the june-bug lights," "the purple from the berries," "lemonade yellow," "green and white," "pink and yellow," "dull orange glow," and shades of red to form a rainbow. This fairy-like imagery suggests a picture of magic and enchantment. But all other colors pale when compared with the magic of blueness. Blue is magic:

> Pretty eyes. Pretty blue eyes. Big blue pretty eyes... Alice has blue eyes. Jerry has blue eyes... They run with their blue eyes. Four blue eyes. Four pretty blue eyes. Blue-sky eyes. Blue like Mrs. Forrest's blue blouse eyes. Morning-glory-blue-eyes. Alice-and-Jerry-blue-storybook eyes. (34-35)

Even the bizarre blue eyes that Pecola saw in the deep silky black cat fascinated her. When she saw them in the light, they shone like blue ice. Even that blueness held an inescapable magic for Pecola.

This blueness, however, becomes even more bizarre when combined with human blackness. It is in this picture that Morrison's irony is apparent. This combination is abnormal and suggestive of the eerie and fearful. It is in this contrast that the absurdity of little black Pecola's desire lies. Perhaps it never occurred to Pecola that Blue eyes in a black face would cause her to be even more rejected than she was in her "normal" situation. Perhaps the absurdity of emphasizing blue eyes did not occur to the editors of the Dick and Jane readers. They simply addressed a Caucasian audience with complete disregard for the black audience upon whom these materials were imposed. For the editors, this black audience simply did not exist. Herein is the bitterest tragic irony of the schizophrenic dilemma of little black Pecolas.

Soaphead Church, Spiritualist and psychic reader, "born with power," fulfills the role of the fairy godmother/father of fairy-tale literature. When Pecola sought his help to change her eyes to blue, she presented him one of his own cards which reads:

> "If you are overcome with trouble and conditions that are not natural, I can remove them; Overcome Spells, Bad Luck and Evil Influences. Remember I am a true Spiritualist and Psychic Reader, born with power, and I will help you. Satisfaction in one visit..." (137)

Pecola's request stymied Soaphead. But Pecola's faith in his ability to "give" her the wish that she longed for was exceeded only by Soaphead's astonishment that someone actually believed in him. Soaphead did not raise his "magic wand" to change Pecola's eyes. Rather in a very poignant and reverential way he raised his hand above her head and made the sign of the Cross. It is in the "magic" of this sign, whatever its irony or fraudulence that the ambiguity lies. Then he acknowledged: "I can do nothing for you my child. I am not a magician. I work only through the Lord. He sometimes uses me to help people. All I can do is offer myself to Him as the instrument through which he works. If He wants your wish granted, He will do it..." (138).

The most profound irony of this situation is that many false fairy godfathers known by such titles as Daddy, Father, and Prophet, and Soaphead Church, exploited the disenchanted of their race and deluded them into believing that they offered the panaceas for their hopelessness and despair. Thousands flocked to their "heavens" and believed that they were saviors. So it is not unthinkable that Pecola Breedlove, a little twelve-year old black girl, was also vulnerable and was deluded enough to believe what she felt so strongly had come to pass — Soaphead Church actually "gave" her blue eyes. The irony of the transformation lies in the comment: "A little black girl yearns for the blue eyes of a little white girl, and the horror at the heart of her yearning is exceeded only by the evil of fulfillment" (162).

In the novel, Toni Morrison skillfully weaves fairy-tale lore into a plot that becomes a horror story rather than a fairy tale. By reversing fairy tale motifs, Morrison creates the horror tale of the psychological dilemma of blacks in a white racist culture. The scenarios that she recounts are familiar to black Americans, but Morrison's approach to the theme makes her plot uniquely her own, resulting in a novel that is deeply profound and hauntingly realistic.

QUESTIONS

1. Discuss some of the advantages and disadvantages of using irony as a narrative technique.

2. Choose passages from *The Bluest Eye* that contrast the real with the make-believe.

3. How do the narrator, Claudia, and her sister, Frieda, complement each other?

4. Choose several of the names of characters in the novel and discuss their allegorical or ironic implications.

5. Define or explain the following terms as they relate to *The Bluest Eye:* Motif, satire, absurdity, negativism, self-denigration.

6. Point out instances of Soaphead Church's fradulence.

7. Discuss the effects of self-denigration on a person's behavior.

8. In what way is Pecola Breedlove a victim of circumstances?

3
VACANT PLACES
SETTING IN THE NOVELS OF TONI MORRISON

A cosmic structure with its basis in the familiar American puritan ethic can be identified in settings in the novels of Toni Morrison. This ethic with its Heaven and Hell is often the panoply against which Morrison's characters improvise their lives — improvise because the traditional law of existence, the Christian ethic itself, for her characters often increases frustration and thereby intensifies their dilemmas. Its requirements of hard work, plenitude, and moral discipline are foiled by the society (Cleanth Brooks and others, *American Literature: The Makers and the Making*, pp. 7-8). Like participants in an ancient, inchoate dance, Morrison's characters create, according to their individual emotions, responses to their milieu, and the resulting rules of expediency are shown against the foil of setting.

The immediate setting of the first three novels is a small midwestern town, the central focus of character and action. Radiating from this center in varying geometric forms are remote ancestral homes, the memories of which are draped in a mixture of the ideal, insecurity, longing and often terror; ideal refuges which are longed for as release from the harshness of life; and temporary havens which blend the real and ideal, but offer no finite resolution to frustrations. In her fourth novel, Morrison chose a Caribbean island as the setting. It contains, however, many of the same elements of the works with American settings, the island lending a concentration of fantasy and magic to the plot.

In *The Bluest Eye* Cholly seems to have emerged from the jaws of Hell to become the hope of Pauline whose background was by comparison idyllic. Pauline is lame, and Morrison utilizes her lameness to symbolize an unconscious susceptibility to evil. She capitulates, in each segment of her environment, to forces both good and evil which erode the lives of her children and herself. Once she is transported to the midwestern town from rural Kentucky, she immerses herself in the imaginary setting of the silver screen, becoming the avitar of her daughter Pecola in yearning to be white and wanting to enjoy the good environment associated with being white. The void of her own world — the bleak storefront home, her deteriorating relationship with Cholly, money problems, and her perception of ugliness in her child — created an environment so frustrating that she could only reflect hatred for her family and herself. Consequently she wrapped herself in a blanket of virtue that was "easy to maintain," and she maintained it to the exclusion of her family. Her gratification took the form of her total absorption in the setting of the white family's home. There she found order. Her other retreat, religion, reinforced the first by providing a rationale or justification for her zealous attention to the needs of the white family and her willful neglect of her own family. The American puritan ethic of hard work and loyalty to one's responsibility was followed assiduously at the house fronting the lake. Pauline's diligence on behalf of the white family was her obedience to God. She saw her own family as an obstruction to her order, including her Christian rectitude. Hence, she was quick to pound into them their sinfulness and unworthiness with the result that her son ran away and her daughter retreated into a pathetic self-hatred that ended in her complete loss of contact with reality.

The emptiness of the setting — its being a "vacant" place — is seen through the device of contrast with the imaginary perfection of family life and place as found in the first grade reader whose characters Dick and Jane, live in attractive, secure surroundings. Morrison's repetitive superimposition of passages from this book emphasizes the starkness of the lives of Pecola and her friends. Two headnotes which open the novel suggest first the fertile abundance in an imaginary textbook setting and secondly the reminder that Marigolds in the real setting of the novel did not grow in the town that year. Vacancy, sterility and futility are conveyed by this description of setting.

In *Sula* Morrison recognizes the rich folk culture in the isolated environment of blacks in the community, but she is keenly aware of the suffocating vacuum which keeps them separated, poor and discouraged. The mound of dirt which stood as a reminder that a bridge was to have been constructed with labor from the Bottom symbolizes the unfulfilled dreams of economic relief.

The theme of vacancy in setting is treated with an irony reflected in the creation of the Bottom where blacks resided. Years before Sula's birth, white townspeople had moved the black population to the Bottom, actually a mountaintop which provided the proper separation the whites desired. As in nearly all such isolated areas, a rich folk culture thrived amid the poverty, violence and often sterile life. The descent from the Bottom was difficult and uncertain; hence, few left except for the strong and defiant ones such as Sula who spent some years in a large city before returning to the Bottom. As in *The Bluest Eye* the juxtaposition of traditional values and immediate needs creates the irony which highlights the actions of the characters. The setting itself is unyielding in the absence of jobs and money. Upon Sula's return to the Bottom, the setting becomes starker as if her presence, with its lack of a morality, places a curse on the area thereby causing wildlife to die and human beings to shrink in fear of her.

The cosmology of *Sula* consists of the Bottom with its footbridge connecting it to the white section of Medallion, the bridge site, and the remote forest with its river where Shadrack the crazed veteran resides. In addition, the large, mysterious cities, such as those seen by Sula, lie far away beckoning the daring.

Nearly every conceivable sin is committed in the Bottom — gambling, whoring, murder, theft, drug addiction and a multitude of other violent acts. They are committed against the background of joblessness and poverty so severe that at one time the only things standing between Eva Peace's family and starvation are two beets. The ambivalence with which the reader is forced to regard Eva's alleged action to get money for her family by letting a train sever one leg is the kind of duality which Morrison elicits from much of the violence which erupts from settings which seethe with such potential. One feels revulsion and sympathy simultaneously. Is Eva Peace a madwoman or a heroine? Morrison creates in this setting a Euripidean fury which springs from the combination of milieu and character.

In her third novel, *Song of Solomon*, Morrison has refined her craft to create a complex setting and cosmogonic system on both the psychological and physical levels. The psychological "climate" exists not only in terms of the burden of racism, but racism as its effects are felt in an isolated environment. This setting in itself spawns much of the action. Yet the longing of Milkman Dead for his real identity establishes the crucial psychological climate of the novel. On the physical level Morrison skillfully weaves a cosmic pattern which encompasses Heaven and Hell and reflects her craftsmanship in its poetry and wholeness.

It is not difficult to identify the Paradise-Hades pattern in Morrison's treatment of physical setting. The images which describe the midwestern town, the Edenic Pennsylvania farm, and the remote cavernous Virginia country are highly suggestive as archetypal symbols. *Song of Solomon* is set in places which correspond to the ideal fecundity and dark caverns of the previous novels. Yet it seems to present deeper association within the reader as the combination of imagery and plot conducts one through the complete cosmogonic cycle. The idea of the cosmogonic cycle is adapted from Joseph Campbell's *Hero with a Thousand Faces*.

Setting in the novels is also enriched by imagery. Maud Bodkin in *Archetypal Patterns* has demonstrated the significance of certain images including mountain-garden, cavern, and river as they reflect the Heaven-Hell pattern. These images are prominent in

Song of Solomon where the microcosm of a Michigan town lies within the macrocosm of the Michigan-Pennsylvania-Virginia universe. For Milkman Dead, his own home, nearby streets and office represent the limited boundaries of his life, and he longs to extend himself beyond them. This "earthbound" environment is complemented by the excursions to their Honore Island beach house with its idyllic setting. In his microcosm, Macon Dead, Milkman's father, regards Honore as heaven and for him it is the ultimate status symbol next to his business, his home and car. Diametrically opposed to his "heaven" is the dark depths of Pilate's winehouse which completes the Heaven-Hell pattern of Milkman's microcosm.

Encircling this smaller universe is the macrocosm consisting of Michigan, Shalimar, Virginia and Montour County, Pennsylvania where Lincoln's Heaven once caressed the first Macon Dead. This heaven has a direct reference back to Solomon's Leap from which old Jake Solomon flew back to his original home. The river which Milkman crossed to reach Solomon's Leap was his last stage of progression from the forested underworld in Virginia to the promontory of heaven.

The emptiness of the microcosm is illustrated in Magdalene's pointing out that the maple tree which she planted in the yard had died. Like the little girls, Frieda and Claudia in *The Bluest Eye*, she places her hope in life on the dependable fertility of nature. When that fails, hope itself fails, for without nature the universe is indeed empty. Yet the emptiness itself might yield something. Pilate's rock collection — each rock taken from one of the places where she was rejected — though worthless, attracts Milkman and Guitar and the collection becomes a talisman which leads Milkman towards his destiny. Hence, even vacant places yield something as long as human beings keep their hopes for the future alive. Morrison places Pilate in her permanent setting, the winehouse, which exudes life and fecundity.

The emptiness is shown, furthermore, by a rhetorical technique in which negatives are juxtaposed with positive values. In *Song of Solomon* blacks called the street on which their one well-to-do physician lived with his family, Doctor Street. When the post office refused to deliver mail to this unofficially named street, and after it served notice that it was not Doctor Street, blacks quickly accepted Not Doctor Street as the name. The negation correlates with the denials in general made by the predominant society against the residents of the town who were black. Similarly, Mercy Hospital, because it would not admit blacks up to the time of Milkman's birth, was called No Mercy Hospital. Hence, life is filled with negation for the black residents of the town, and these negative elements represent the absence of meaning in the language used by the dominant society.

Significant also in Morrison's treatment of setting in her novels is what Maud Bodkin calls the "magic of place-names." A portion of Bodkin's review of observations on place names made by writers of phychological insight follows:

> Marcel Proust has described vividly the effect of certain place-names upon the mind of an imaginative child. An unknown place becomes, he says, individual by having, like a person, a name for itself alone. Some character in the sound of the name, together with fragments of description assimilated in connection with it, would give rise, Proust tells us, in his childish fancy, to a vision unique, and as personal as love for a human being. An accumulated store of dreams was "magnetized" by the name, so that the place behind the name seemed "a thing for which my soul was athirst."...Within the name was enclosed the magic of "the life not yet lived," of "Life intact and pure." It is such an illusion of the very life of life awaiting one at some point within the unknown that has lured travellers forth to distant lands; and the same readiness of our dreams to be magnetized by place-names has given to these a distinctive value and power in poetry. (102)

The second Macon Dead remembered his idyllic early life at Lincoln's Heaven. The Pennsylvania farm, acquired after his father attained his freedom, was the longed for Eden which provided a secure and prosperous family life. As Eden, it was earthbound, for it collapsed with the murder of the first Macon Dead. Yet its memory, transmitted to his grandchildren, caused Milkman Dead to yearn for it and the purity of life that the mere name elicited. Its magic widened his aspirations to seek the longed for Edenic flight at Solomon's Leap, a place-name which carries the highest human longing of not only the descendants of Solomon, but of all the blacks in Milkman Dead's milieu. Shalimar, in Virginia, is itself the affectionately corrupt version of Solomon, the name which was so "magnetized" that it drew to it a song and children's game which contained those fragments needed by Milkman to possess a vision of his origin, the place to which he was compelled to go for his ultimate personal fulfillment.

In *Sula*, the significance of names is evident in the ancestral home of Nel on Elysian Fields Street in New Orleans. This home remained a memory of the enchanting smell of gardenias for Nel who was too young, upon returning there for her great grandmother's funeral, to know that her own mother was the daughter of a creole whore who worked at Sundown House with its red shutters. The mother's refuge was the house on Elysian Fields where high morality was practiced and which was guarded by "the dolesome eyes of a multicolored Virgin Mary, counseling her to be constantly on guard for any sign of her mother's wild blood" (17). From the house on Elysian Fields Nel's mother went to Medallion to live a conservative life against the moral dangers that might beset her daughter. The names Elysian Fields and Sundown House suggest the moral spectrum of Paradise-Hades.

In addition, Medallion as a name suggests something memorialized, and it is obviously intended to tie in with the attraction for the incidents related to National Suicide Day and the veteran Shadrack. Furthermore, memories, both gentle and terrible, become a large part of the plot which takes place in ity in Son, and her aunt and uncle seeing their true relationship to the Streets. The island with its enchantment was concomitantly disturbing and evoked the dark areas of the psyche which revealed some truths, long masked, that were not pleasant to encounter. They included memories, dreams, magic and ritual. All of these elements deserve more specific treatment of the important ways in which they are utilized in the development of the novel. In brief, they are each combined with images of nature — landscape and animal images — to reflect the unlimited richness and fertility of a prelapsarian paradise.

Setting in Toni Morrison's novels can be described against the foil of the American puritan ethic with its inherent discipline and against the "norm" of the white society which is constantly visible as an economic and social backdrop to the problems confronted by her characters. The milieu of the whites often serves to emphasize the emptiness of setting in these works. Yet Morrison's characters emerge as persons in a realistic world which is often reconstructed to form that which can be utilized for living. The alternative to such re-creating is death of the spirit. Survival in spirit, a goal which underlies all her novels, is the heroic result of creating in a vacuum. Setting, therefore, is an antagonist, a character itself, which possesses countless means of stifling the ideals and yearnings of other characters.

QUESTIONS

1. Is it possible to identify with two worlds at once as Morrison's characters are forced to do? Explain your answer.

2. If setting is a powerful "character" imposing its will on individuals, which characters evoke your sympathy and which ones evoke condemnation?

3. The problem of textbook relevance for all segments of American society is posed in *The Bluest Eye*. What solutions to this issue would you offer?

4. Name other instances in which traditional values clash with immediate reality in Morrison's work or in society as you view it.

5. Is the sterility of the isolated environment in Morrison's novel(s) justification for the integration of all ethnic groups in our society?

6. Despite the emptiness of their setting, certain characters hold tenaciously to a hope or an ideal. Why is this possible?

7. Are the rhetorical elements treated in the essay typical of the language of blacks or is this use of them merely a stylistic device?

4 Psychological Disorientation In SULA

When one reads *Sula*, it becomes immediately apparent that Toni Morrison used psychological disorientation as both a stylistic and thematic device to make the reader aware of existing presuppositions as well as cause him to examine his own perceptions of reality. Names of places, people and events become a part of Morrison's rhetorical strategy whereby she presents and suggests certain attitudes towards human relationships. As in *The Bluest Eye*, in *Sula* Morrison is concerned with the complexities of life during the first part of the twentieth century when times were difficult for many Americans, but most especially for black Americans regardless of the part of the country in which they lived. It is against this frame of reference that one must view much of the psychological disorientation in *Sula*.

The scene of the action in *Sula* is in the Bottom, the black section of Medallion, Ohio. The designation "Bottom" is not an unusual one for the black section of town especially if it is low-lying topographically, near the river front or in other ways sharply distinct from the white section of town. The irony of the designation in *Sula*, however, is that the Bottom is high up in the hills. The "nigger joke" that explains the origin of the name also explains one aspect of the psychological disorientation in the novel. The white farmer who promised the slave his freedom and a piece of bottom land if he would execute a difficult task perpetrated a cruel hoax on the slave by telling him that the hills were "bottom land, rich and fertile." The farmer's statement so disoriented the slave that he really believed that the hills were the Bottom, and so "the nigger got the hilly land, where planting was backbreaking, where the soil slid down and washed away the seeds, and where the wind lingered all through the winter" (5).

When a "nigger joke" is told by blacks to other blacks, it has a different meaning than when told by blacks to whites, whites to blacks or whites to whites. When blacks tell a "nigger joke" to other blacks, the irony never escapes the black audience, but it is not always immediately apparent to other audiences. A similar situation is seen in much of the black folklore in jokes and tales concerning why blacks have dark skin, curly hair and the like. The blacks always attribute their situation to what to non-blacks would appear to be racial stupidity, huge ignorances or maybe even laziness. What blacks are doing, however, is far more subtle than is immediately apparent. They are using the white man's perception of blacks to psychologically disorient him and thereby proceed to feign an attitude that allows them to do and say much more than is being perceived by the white man.

Although the Bottom was high up in the hills and the white farmer thought that his mesmerizing the slave had been to his advantage, and perhaps it was then, it also had a psychological advantage for the slave as well as blacks who lived in the Bottom many years later. By psychologically disorienting himself, the slave could endure the hardships that he faced and survive the cruel vicissitudes of his existence. It allowed blacks in later years to be critical of their surroundings without risking mistreatment as a result. For the blacks in Medallion, Ohio, in 1919 and the years leading up to and through the Great Depression, the Bottom designated much more than the irony of the physical site. It had more to do with their sociological, psychological and economic plight. Blacks were indeed at rock bottom compared to other Americans. Therefore, it is not unthinkable that they had to become schizophrenic to a degree to survive. Morrison uses the psychological disorientation inherent in naming the hills the Bottom to subtly address the tragic dilemma of blacks in white American society in the same way that Maxim Gorky speaks of the lower depths when discussing the poor and oppressed classes in nineteenth century Russian society.

An interesting footnote to the irony of the Bottom is that the area quietly became known as the suburbs when "they tore the nightshade and blackberry patches from their roots to make room for the Medallion City Golf Course..." (1). The "roots" of the "nightshade and blackberry patches" were unimportant to the white suburbanites, a tragic commentary on what happens to black neighborhoods and black culture in America.

A final observation regarding the Bottom is that the white farmer's hoax boomeranged inasmuch as the "hunters who went there sometimes wondered in private if maybe the white farmer was right after all. Maybe it was the bottom of heaven" (6). By attempting to disorient blacks, whites themselves often become victims of their own schemes.

The commemoration of National Suicide Day also reflects a kind of psychological disorientation. When Shadrack instituted January third as National Suicide Day in 1920, it appeared to be just another crazy prank of the young black World War I private who was suffering from shellshock. "Telling them that this was their only chance to kill themselves or each other" (14), Shadrack rang his cowbell and carried his hangman's rope as he summoned the crowd together. For Shadrack the celebration was an opportunity for folk to spend one day a year sorting out the problems of death and dying so that they could be free from those thoughts for the rest of the year. In other words, the celebration of National Suicide Day was a catharsis of a sort, a purging, as it were, in the Aristotelian sense, of their thoughts regarding suicide and death. The "normal" people in the town who were initially fearful of and frightened by Shadrack's parades gradually altered their mental attitudes:

> As time went along, the people took less notice of these January thirds, or rather they thought they did, though they had no attitudes or feelings one way or another about Shadrack's solitary parade. In fact they had simply stopped remarking on the holiday because they had absorbed it into their thoughts, into their language, into their lives...

> Easily, quietly, Suicide Day became a part of the
> fabric of life up in the Bottom of Medallion, Ohio.
> (15-16)

In short, the people of the Bottom became psychologically disoriented and Shadrack appeared to have designed a "sane" scheme.

The three Deweys represent a special kind of mental disorientation. When they came to live with Eva Peace, each at different times, Eva did not hesitate to call they all Dewey. It did not matter that Dewey One was black with jaundiced eyes, that Dewey Two was light-skinned, red-headed and freckled, and that Dewey Three was half-Mexican, nor that they were one or two years apart in age. Eva Peace simply commented, "'What you need to tell them apart for. They's all dewey'" (38). When Eva made that comment, no one foresaw the truth of her prophecy. It was not long before these unrelated orphans became a trinity losing their individuality and functioning as one mind.

The disbelieving teacher who taught them in the first grade finally accepted Eva's logic regarding their names and ages, "for she had long ago given up trying to fathom the ways of the colored people in town" (38), and she became a victim of the "they all look alike" syndrome:

> ....she gradually found that she could not tell one from the other. The deweys would not allow it. They got all mixed up in her head, and finally she could not literally believe her eyes. They spoke with one voice, thought with one mind, and maintained an annoying privacy. Stouthearted, surly and wholly unpredictable, the deweys remained a mystery not only during all of their lives in Medallion but after as well. (39)

Eva's logic regarding the Deweys may be attributed to her not wanting to show preference or greater favoritism for one over the other. It appears that she wished to maintain as much emotional detachment as possible in her relationship with them. When the first Dewey came, she looked closely at "his wrists, the shape of his head and the temperament that showed in his eyes and said, 'Well. Look at Dewey. My my mymymy'" (37). Eva's comment after the third Dewey was brought by his mother to her house was similar to her reaction to the first Dewey. Her seeming disorientation appears to be a tactic that would enable her to cope with the apparent desertion of three little boys. Conversely, the teacher's psychological disorientation appears to be a result of her not being willing "to fathom the ways of the colored people of the town," not being willing to understand the black psyche. The chasm between her and the boys was symbolic of the wider chasm between the black people of the Bottom and the white people in the other parts of Medallion, Ohio.

As the years went by the three Deweys remained a mystery to everybody remaining much the same in stature, mind and temperament as they were when they came to live with Eva. Finally, they died, at least it was supposed, during a National Suicide Day parade. The irony is that they were as indistinct in death as they were in life.

The years before the three Deweys came to live with Eva Peace, she had given a small room to a mountain boy who looked half-white although Eva said he was "all white." Ironically, Eva called him Tar Baby out of a mixture of fun and meanness. Medallion, Ohio, in 1920 was a segregated community and the only way that blacks could cope with a white man in the Bottom was to mentally disorient themselves and verbally reverse his racial identity. This appears to be a part of the logic of Eva's designation. Black humor is frequently more subtle than is suspected by the outsider. Black humor has very little to do with being funny. It generally is the black person's way of undergoing psychological disorientation, and it has a great deal to do with things "far more deeply interfused."

Though the blacks accepted Tar Baby without consideration of race, the whites could not accept his reversed racial role maintaining that he "should come down out of those hills and live like a decent white man" (133). Tar Baby himself was able to cope with his situation by drinking himself to death and singing in the sweetest hill voice imaginable "In the Sweet By and By" at Wednesday night prayer meeting. Ironically, the church women who listened to his song wept as they heard him sing as they had graphic thoughts of their own imminent deaths. But the paradox is that they were indifferent to Tar Baby's spiritual dilemma. The dichotomy of his life and his song did not cause them to live out their Christianity by encouraging him to try to pick up the broken pieces of his life. It appears that the women had psychologically disoriented themselves to the point that they could mentally deny any guilt or responsibility for not helping Tar Baby to improve his own spiritual outlook.

Whatever Tar Baby's psychological orientation, he met death in the same way that the three Deweys did during a celebration of National Suicide Day. The irony of his situation is that he had already committed suicide a bit day by day. But society paid no heed to his condition. Conversely, society is oriented to think of certain kinds of behavior as damaging to one's person or well-being and disoriented to recognizing all other forms of self-destruction.

Eva Peace, whose home was a boarding house where all sorts of people dropped in, is a striking example of how one can become psychologically disoriented and behave in ways that she herself considers normal and thereby suffer no apparent guilt for her actions. As already pointed out, she took the three Deweys and Tar Baby into her home and underwent some psychological disorientation in the process. However, the most bizarre instance of her disorientation was the "coup de grace" that she committed on her own son Plum. During the act, Plum, too, became disoriented. When Eva awakened him from the rim of light sleep by dousing him with kerosene,

> He felt twilight. Now there seemed to be some kind of wet light traveling over his legs and stomach with a

> deeply attractive smell. It would itself — this wet
> light — all about him, splashing and running into his
> skin. He opened his eyes and saw what he imagined was
> the great wing of an eagle pouring a wet lightness over
> him. Some kind of baptism, some kind of blessing, he
> thought. Everything is going to be all right, it said.
> Knowing that it was, he closed his eyes and sank back
> into the bright hope of sleep.   (47)

Because of her mentally distorted condition, Eva Peace could go back to her room and put herself to bed even while Plum burned because she was disoriented into accepting her actions as an act of grace. Even while Plum burned to death, Eva could mentally deny any guilt or responsibility and simply ask, "Is? My baby? Burning?"

On the other hand, later when Eva saw Hannah afire in the yard and the flames licking her blue dress and making her dance, she smashed the windowpane of her second floor room and threw herself out the window. Again, Eva's mind became distorted. Paradoxically, she became sufficiently mentally distorted to murder Plum, her baby, while conversely, she could become do disoriented that she would jump from her second floor window to save the life of Hannah, her firstborn.

Eva's orientation towards the psychologically abnormal began long before she administered Plum's "coup de grace" or tried unsuccessfully to save Hannah's life. Earlier, she had exhibited a kind of abnormality in laying her leg on the railroad track for the train to run over in order to get insurance money to take care of her family which had been deserted by BoyBoy, her husband. When one considers the horrors of that act and the accompanying pain that Eva underwent in order that she and her family could survive, it is highly conceivable that she could sufficiently disorient herself to do anything else that she felt necessary. Perhaps Nel best expressed Eva's state of mind in the comment that she made when she visited Eva in Sunnydale Nursing Home many years later, "You're con- fused, Miss Peace..." (168).

The most profound instance of psychological disorientation in *Sula* is exhibited in the main character of the novel, Sula Peace. An aura of disorientation and confusion surrounded Sula from her birth. She was born with a strange black mark over her eye that looked like a stem and rose to Nel, a copperhead to Jude, and "Hannah's ashed marking her from the very beginning" (114) to everybody else in town. All of her life in the Bottom Sula lived in a woolly house where the women loved maleness and some touching everyday. Judging by the surroundings in which she grew up, it would be expected that Sula would behave differently from even her best friend, the other part of her equation, Nel Wright. And so Sula created both fear and wonder in the minds of the townspeople who recognized that she

> ... was distinctly different. Eva's arrogance and Hannah's self-indulgence merged in her and, with a twist of that was all her own imagination, she lived out her days exploring her own thoughts and emotions, giving them full reign, feeling no obligation to please nobody unless their pleasure pleased her. As willing to give pain as to feel pain, to feel pleasure as to give pleasure, hers was an experimental life — ever since her mother's remark sent her flying up those stairs, ever since her one major feeling of responsibility had been exorcised on the bank of a river with a closed place in the middle... She had no center, no speck around to grow... She was completely free of ambitions, with no affection for money, property or things, no greed, no desire to command attention or compliments — no ego. For that reason she felt no compulsion to verify herself — be consistent with herself. (118-119)

Indeed, Sula was different. Whether by the circumstances of her birth or the influence of her woolly environment, she exhibited an uncanny craziness and strangeness that not only reflected themselves in what she did and said, but in what she caused others to do any say. Sula's difference was recognized by others when she was only twelve years old when she slashed off the tip of her finger to prove to four teen-aged white boys what punishment she could inflict on them if they did not stop harassing her and Nel: "'If I can do that to myself, what you suppose I'll do to you'" (55)? Later, the girl that neither gnats nor mosquitoes would settle on in what was supposedly a playful gesture

> picked [Chicken Little] up by his hands and swung him outward then around and around. His knickers ballooned and his shrieks of frightened joy startled the birds and the fat grasshoppers. When he slipped from her hands and sailed away out over the water they could still hear his bubbly laughter.
>
> The water darkened and closed quickly over the place where Chicken Little sank. The pressure of his hand and tight little fingers was still in Sula's palms as she stood looking at the closed place in the water. They expected him to come back up, laughing. Both girls stared at the water. (61)

Sula's bizarre strangeness is exhibited in her not making any attempt to save Chicken's life. She simply "watched" as in the expression "deathwatch." Similarly, she "watched" her own mother "Hannah burn not because she was paralyzed, but because she was interested" (78). Years later when she herself lay dying she confessed, "I stood there watching her burn and was thrilled. I wanted her to keep on jerking like that, to keep on dancing" (149).

When Sula returned to Medallion, Ohio, after a ten-year absence, a plague of robins accompanied her. Whether Sula was the cause or effect of the robins' being in Medallion or even whether it was simply coincidental that the robins and Sula came into town at the same time is debatable. Nevertheless, the appearance of the robins suggested to the townspeople that Sula had power over external nature also. The signs in nature supported their beliefs in Sula's preternaturalness as Eva commented upon Sula's return, "'I might have knowed them birds meant something'" (91).

The townspeople's belief in Sula's ability to distort reality was supported by other incidents such as her looking at Teapot and his falling down the steps, her looking at Mr. Finley and his swallowing a chicken bone and dying on the spot, her looking at Shadrack and his tipping his hat, and her looking at Dessie and a sty coming on her eye. Incidentally or coincidentally, Sula's strangeness and craziness had an uncanny effect on the people of the Bottom and resulted in their own psychological distortion:

> In their world, aberrations were as much a part of nature as grace. It was not for them to expel or annihilate it. They would no more run Sula out of town than they would kill the robins that brought her back, for in their secret awareness of Him, He was not the God of three faces they sang about. They knew quite well that He had four, and the fourth explained Sula.   (118)

Sula's mental distortion regarding who she was and who Nel was is probably the most tragic aspect of her psychological disorientation: "She had clung to Nel as the closest thing to both an other and a self, only to discover that she and Nel were not one and the same thing" (119). Her rude awakening came when she bedded down with Nel's husband Jude and the heartbreak that she inflicted upon Nel. But ironically, after Sula's death Nel's mental state became as disoriented as Sula's:

> "All the time, all that time, I thought I was missing Jude.' And the loss pressed down on her chest and came up into her throat. 'We was girls together; she said as though explaining something. 'O Lord, Sula,' she cried, 'girl, girl, girlgirlgirl."   (174)

Certain signs after Sula's death further support the belief that she was a witch. Particularly, blacks were hired to work on the tunnel spanning the river and construction began on the new old folks' home, indications that God's mighty thumb had been at Sula's throat and that the source of their own evil had been confirmed.

"Playing crazy" is a tactic that has often been attributed to blacks in their attempt to maintain a certain degree of privacy when dealing with whites and sometimes indifferent blacks, but Morrison's *Sula* strongly implies that "playing crazy" is only one way to address the problem of survival. In order to survive life in the Bottom of Medallion, Ohio, and in the other bottoms of society, it is often necessary for blacks to possess a dual consciousness, as it were, disoriented in mind and attitude and view life from both the normal and the opposite point of what is perceived as normality. Life in the Bottom of Medallion, Ohio, was hard, and the people's survival depended on their ability to find a point on both the philosophical and psychological compass that would allow them to maintain and unswerving faith in God's justice even in the midst of hardship and misery. How else could they survive

> ... failed crops, ... rednecks, lost jobs, sick children, rotten potatoes, broken pipes, bug-ridden flour, third-class coal, educated social workers, thieving insurance men, garlic-ridden hunkies, corrupt Catholics, racist Protestants, cowardly Jews, slaveholding Moslems, jackleg nigger preachers, squeamish Chinamen, cholera, dropsy or the Black Plague, let along a strange woman.... (150)

QUESTIONS

1. Enumerate some of Sula's unusual physical and mental characteristics.

2. What are some of the effects of psychological disorientation on a person's perception of reality?

3. Do you consider Eva Peace to be heroic in any way? Why? Why not?

4. Discuss the pervading mood of *Sula*.

5. Do you feel that Sula's unusual background and characteristics should justify her escaping the censure of the townspeople of Medallion, Ohio? Why? Why not?

6. How is folklore used to reinforce the narrative?

7. How do you account for the appearance of the birds when Sula returns home? Is this event symbolic in any way?

8. Discuss other examples of symbolism in the novel.

9. What does the novel appear to say implicitly or explicitly about life, happiness, and hope?

5
PILATE DEAD: CONJURESS

In each of Toni Morrison's novels a character emerges who is capable of transforming illusion into reality and of affecting, as if by magic, the realities of other characters in his milieu. Soaphead Church in *The Bluest Eye*, Shadrach in *Sula*, Pilate in *Song of Solomon* and Son in *Tar Baby* have the ability to summon, obtain and mysteriously convey the objects of the earnest quests made by alienated and despairing persons. They are agents of metamorphosis whose inspired visions of the past give them supernatural insight into the present and future. Their function in the novels is that of interpreters, and more precisely, critics of ideals and realities which emanate from their environment. In addition, they give meaning to absurd elements in the narratives. Finally, as agents of change, they hold the keys to questions addressed in the respective plots.

This chapter will analyze the function of Pilate in *Song of Solomon* as she is seen through the multiple viewpoints of other characters, through her role as conjuress with its affective power on others; and through her effective vision which becomes the source of meaning in the novel.

Using a technique reminiscent of William Faulkner, Toni Morrison permits no unilateral view of Pilate in revealing her character. It is only through the combined viewpoints of Macon Dead, Ruth Dead, Milkman and Circe that one approximates a reasonable perception of Morrison's most enigmatic character. The novel has done its own work of identifying the grotesque in its key characters. What remains to be answered is the question of the final achievement of the novel. One answer is the unique function of the character who serves as the matrix of the plot — Pilate Dead.

Pilate's first appearance in the novel is as one of numerous witnesses at Robert Smith's spectacular jump from Mercy Hospital. She is oddly dressed in a navy cap and a multicolored quilt. Even during this earliest action in the plot, Pilate is interpreting events. While Smith stands poised on the roof of the hospital, clothed as a shaman in magical costume with his makeshift wings, Pilate's voice is heard singing "Sugarman done fly away/ Sugarman done gone/ Sugarman cut across the sky/ Sugarman gone home..." (6). If her song is to be interpreted as commentary on the spectacle, it is a knowing, approving commentary which accepts the event as complacently as the flight of birds in migration. Her song floats antiphonally smooth against the moans of Ruth Dead and the coarse shouts of other spectators. The result is that Morrison has established imagery of flight as a fundamental element in the novel. The reader realizes upon completing the novel that the flight of Pilate's ancestor, Solomon, is the original one and that Robert Smith is one of numerous symbols of Solomon, a totem figure which functions as a paradigm of the loss and rebirth of the culture. The Robert Smith spectacle serves furthermore as the mechanism for introducing the conjurative powers of Pilate. A moment before Smith's jump, and using an image of flight, she foretold the time of Ruth's delivery.

> A little bird'll be here with the morning... The women were looking deep into each other's eyes when a loud roar went up from the crowd-- a kind of wavy sound. Mr. Smith had lost his balance for a second, and was trying gallantly to hold on to a triangle of wood that jutted from the cupola. Immediately the singing woman began again:
> O Sugarman done fly/ O Sugarman done gone... Mr. Smith... heard the music, and leaped on into the air.
> (9)

In addition to her seeing into the future, Pilate confirms with her song the rightness of Smith's flight. For he had tried to hold onto the cupola before her song reached his ears, a suggestion that her power to activate the flight was all that was needed at that moment.

The birth of the novel's hero the next day begins an interplay of present and past actions which define

Pilate's significance to the plot as a conjuress and more significantly as the supernatural aid in Milkman's heroic quest. Her miraculous birth, random naming and sudden appearance in the town represent an unconventional set of circumstances which lend a mystery to the character whom the novel never completely reveals. To Macon Dead, her brother, she was an object of shame with her unkempt appearance, eccentricities and her illegal manufacture and selling of wine. Macon recalled her appearance in the city a year before Milkman's birth. To the reader the timeliness of her appearance suggests possible intuitive powers which pointed Pilate, after years of separation, to her brother's city. She hovered around his wife Ruth during her pregnancy and after Milkman's birth until "Finally he told her not to come again until she could show some respect for herself. Could get a real job instead of running a wine house" (20). Artfully depicted, Pilate's wine house becomes a symbol early in the novel of her intoxicating power over the many blacks who buy her wine. In the years to come this power would be extended to Macon's son. A foreshadowing of this occurred when Macon could not understand the intense expression on Pilate's face as she sat near the crib with a "surprise" and "eagerness" that made Macon uneasy. This established the initial bond between Milkman and Pilate-- a bond which would carry them all the way to Solomon's Leap. Macon's reverie about Pilate was interrupted by the news that one of his tenants, Porter, had perched himself in an attic window and was waving a shotgun. Macon realized that only Pilate could have sold Porter any liquor. Porter's precarious stance revives the flight image initiated by Robert Smith. It also reaffirms Pilate's ability to unleash her power to make men fly from their earthbound plight. While Morrison conveys these events through Macon Dead, Macon himself is unaware of their significance, for he can only concentrate on protecting his money and his reputation. Hence, the power he wields is as tangible as money and real estate and it serves as a useful foil for the supernatural power which his sister holds. Macon takes a short cut home upon returning from the Porter spectacle, and he finds himself on Darling Street where Pilate lived "in a narrow single-story house whose basement seemed to be rising from rather than settling into the ground" (27). The rising quality of the house is consistent with Pilate's own emergence into the world as Macon recalls Pilate's birth as he stood in the darkness near her house.

> After their mother died, she had come struggling out of the womb without help from throbbing muscles or pressure of swift womb water. As a result, for all the years he knew her, her stomach was as smooth and sturdy as her back, at no place interrupted by a navel. It was the absence of a navel that convinced people that she had not come into this world through normal channels; had never lain, floated, or grown in some warm and liquid place connected by a tissue - this tube to a reliable course of human nourishment. (27-28)

Pilate "inched" her own way out of her dead mother's womb and once her umbilical cord was cut, it fell off leaving no trace of its existence. Her miraculous birth is thus made more mysterious by what may be called Pilate's personal diaspora in which she began her life cut off and would continue to have a series of severances until her instinctive search ended with Milkman. As he walked by her house, Macon is drawn by Pilate's singing. He even makes another trip to her house after going to his own home which, by contrast, was void of music. He heard Pilate leading "a phrase that the other two were taking up and building on. Her powerful contralto, Reba's piercing soprano in counterpoint, and the soft voice of the girl, Hagar... pulled him like a carpet tack under the influence of a magnet" (29). Even Macon was not immune to Pilate's power to summon. As he peeped through a window, he consciously observed the physical disorder in which they lived, but he surrendered to the sound which evoked the past and made him think of "fields and wild turkey and calico." As she led the singing, stirring her wine pulp, she was officiant, priestess of an ageless ritual that transported Macon to a past which included the serene life which he and Pilate led in a remote Pennsylvania paradise. His viewpoint is utilized by Morrison to give the first rendering of the initial stage of Pilate's ontogeny-- her beginning even before birth a personal history which is analogous to the diaspora of blacks and the numerous times they were cut off-- recapitulating the experience of the race as a whole. Pilate is thus an archetypal symbol which transcends ethnicity; she is not only the wanderer of legend, but also the wise woman of myth who guides those who search for lost fields. Obviously, through Macon Dead the reader sees more of Pilate than Macon is capable of seeing. For example, when he recalled his father's method of naming Pilate by randomly placing his finger on a word in the Bible, he introduced unconsciously an ambiguous question. The midwife, in protesting the choice of Pilate as a name, reminded the illiterate father that Pilate was "no riverboat pilot" but a Christ-killing Pilate. The father replied simply that he had "asked Jesus to save me my wife." Macon reveals, as he reflects on this aspect of Pilate's birth, that Pilate's life was a departure from convention, and not only that, but her name, though randomly chosen, was an immediate antagonism against Christ who had not saved her mother, the wife of the first Macon Dead. Through Macon's memory, Pilate's motherless arrival into the world did not overshadow the unanswered prayer of his father. Macon seemed to regard his own life as self-progenitored and self-centered, for his selfishness throughout the novel is ironically contrasted with the self abnegating acts of Pilate.

Macon later told his twelve year old son some details of his childhood with Pilate. Yet he remonstrated against Milkman's going to Pilate's house because he considered her to be a snake" ...and can charm you like a snake, but still a snake" (54). Some years later Macon learned of a green sack, supposedly containing gold which Milkman informed him was hanging in Pilate's house. By this time Milkman had become

Hagar's lover and a regular visitor at Pilate's wine house. The green sack stimulated Macon to tell the rest of his life story beginning this time with the whites who murdered his father for his land. Macon and Pilate, having witnessed the murder, fled — a second diaspora for Pilate. He remembered Circe, the midwife, hiding them in the huge mansion of the family for whom she worked. It was here that Pilate, aided by Circe, took a little brass box which had belonged to her mother and put the scrap of paper containing her name in it and, after a Negro blacksmith soldered wire to it, put it through her earlobe. Pilate's name encaged in the box is symbolic of her yearning to take, perhaps through others, the ancestral flight. Pilate's third flight soon followed as she and Macon headed for Virginia where Macon thought they had people.

Their flight was interrupted by the apparition of their father sitting on a stump. That night, taking refuge in a cave, Macon killed a white man, discovered gold and saw once more an apparition of his father who whispered "Sing. Sing." Pilate refused to take the gold which resulted in a fight erupting between them. Driving Macon from the cave with the knife he had just used to kill the white man, Pilate's threat kept him away from the cave for three days. Upon returning, he found that the gold and Pilate were gone. In recalling this part of his life, Macon clarified his use of the snake image in describing Pilate. His erroneous belief, for more than twenty years, that she had taken the gold after turning on him to keep him from taking it, inflamed his hatred. By the time that Macon progresses to this stage in his reminiscence, the reader is aware that his insatiable greed for wealth dominates him. He shared the story with Milkman for the single purpose of enlisting his help in retrieving the green sack at Pilate's house. The cave, for Macon, became an underworld in which his loving little sister became transformed into a monstrous guardian of the gates of Hell. This alienation of brother and sister becomes Morrison's device for invoking the total and final separation from family and other people which Pilate was to endure throughout her youth. Moreover, the recurrent apparition of her father heightens the alienation with its mysterious two-word admonition.

Macon's reflections on Pilate omit much of what is recalled by his wife Ruth Dead who remembers that it was Pilate's conjurative power which increased Macon's sexual desire and thus enabled her to have her third child, Milkman. She had used "...the nasty greenish-gray powder Pilate had given her to be stirred into rain water and put into food" (131). The atrocities committed by Macon in his attempts to make her abort had sent Ruth again to Pilate for help. Ruth, in reviewing those years, told Milkman of Pilate's arrival. "...and soon as she saw me she knew what my trouble was. And she asked me one day, 'Do you want him?' "I want somebody,' I told her. He ought to have a son. Otherwise this be the end of us'" (125). Her voodoo powers notwithstanding, Pilate's role as heroine fulfilling a need is more directly described by Ruth than any other character. Pilate reveals the sources of her conjurative powers to Ruth when the latter visits her. Her aid against the violent Macon is immediate.

> She also told her not to worry. Macon wouldn't bother her no more; she, Pilate, would see to it. (Years later Ruth learned that Pilate put a small doll on Macon's chair in his office. A male doll with a small painted chicken bone stuck between its legs and a round red circle painted on its belly. Macon knocked it out of the chair and with a yardstick pushed it into the bathroom, where he doused it with alcohol and burned it. It took nine separate burnings before the fire got down to the straw and cotton ticking of its insides. But he must have remembered the round fire-red stomach, for he left Ruth alone after that). (132)

Again Macon is forced to submit to Pilate's power. There is no doubt that Macon knows the source of the doll. Yet he is unable to counter its magic.

In assessing Pilate, Ruth knew that her "equilibrium overshadowed all her eccentricities" and she broke years of Macon's imposed alienation to get Pilate's aid once more in saving Milkman's life — this time from Hagar. Morrison uses a series of short sentences which contrast Pilate and Ruth and which underlines the paradox of their harmonious relationship.

> "One black, the other lemony. One corseted, the other buck naked under her dress. One well read but ill traveled. The other had read only a geography book, but had been from one end of the country to another. One wholly dependent on money for life, the other indifferent to it. But those were the meaningless things. Their similarities were profound. Both were vitally interested in Macon Dead's son, and both had close and supportive posthumous communication with their fathers." (139)

It is obvious that Pilate needed no bond with Ruth other than Milkman who must continue the Dead name. Perhaps this explains Pilate's openness in discussing supernatural occurrences with her sister-in-law. Morrison utilizes this openness to reveal the origin of Pilate's power.

First Pilate describes the visitations from her father and, in contrast to Macon who simply dismissed them as unusual phenomena, she indicates how these visitations sustained her throughout her alienated life. She reveals that he instructed her by pointing her in the right direction. Hence her subsequent diaspora was not randomly chosen.

Thus Ruth is important as a receptacle of knowledge about Pilate and through her an illuminating facet of Pilate's character is developed as Pilate narrates a series of severances from other people. "I was cut off from people early...When I cut out by myself, I headed for Virginia" (141). En route to Virginia she stopped with a preacher's family, but she was put out when the preacher made advances. A three-year stay with migrant workers followed and the woman who took her in was a root worker who "taught me a lot." Here another source of her power is given. She was cut off a fourth time when it was learned that she had no navel, for the root worker told her that a navel is "for people who were born natural" (143). Hence, the women among the migrant workers saw Pilate as "something God never made." She found another migrant group, but one day they left her while she was in town buying thread. She had slept with a man who discovered her smooth belly. The image of thread is highly suggestive of her desire to be tied to something. But her fifth diaspora was accomplished, and possessing only a geography book and rocks collected on her migrant wanderings, she took up residence in a laundry until she had saved enough to go south by wagon. Her actual trip to Virginia, her sixth cutting off, found her arriving in Culpepper where no one knew of the Dead family. Leaving Culpepper, she went to an Island off the Virginia coast where she became pregnant and refused to marry the man fearing that he would one day discover that she had no navel. Her isolation is sealed, therefore, by a physical defect which determines the course her life will take.

Shortly after her child's birth, and instructed by her father, Pilate returned to Pennsylvania to collect the bones of the murdered white man. Even at this stage, Pilate accepts her conjurative powers without question. She had not taken part in the murder, but accepted responsibility for it. Returning to Virginia a month later with a sack and remaining on the island with Reba until she was two years old, she wandered once more, an eighth cutting off. Pilate told Ruth how her smooth abdomen isolated her. "...denied her: partnership in marriage, confessional friendship, and communal religion... When she realized what her situation in the world was and would probably always be she threw away every assumption she had learned and began at zero" (148-149). This knowledge freed Pilate to shed the trappings of convention and she feared nothing.

Having lived a life of severances, Pilate thus had an "alien's compassion for troubled people" in spite of the treatment she received at the hands of people who feared her. Pilate, as conjure woman, was subjected often to counter-conjure by the women who swept up her footprints or put mirrors on her door. As a result, she continued to live from town to town working as a bootlegger. It was after the birth of Reba's daughter Hagar that she decided to find her brother Macon, for Hagar "needed family" and a more conventional life, and Pilate wanted to "make peace" with her brother.

Once there she settled permanently, against her natural inclination to wander, to help Ruth who was "dying of lovelessness." Pilate's version of her life ends with her expression of an unselfish love for the alienated, characterized by Ruth Dead, who can be identified with the tragic mulatto of literature with her light skin and her social standing, and who is isolated from other blacks. This desolation as with any form of alienation touched the compassionate Pilate. With her own life lived as a series of severances, she has been the homeless wanderer whose only hope for return rests in Milkman. Thus Ruth serves an important function in the novel. She becomes the medium through which Pilate defines herself in isolation.

Toni Morrison's hero, Milkman, is also an important means of defining Pilate. His encounters with her demonstrate the irrevocable bond between them and reveal other aspects of her power to perform magic. Through Milkman Pilate is revealed as a conjure woman after the theft of the green sack from her house. Milkman and his friend Guitar, arrested for the theft, are freed by the testimony of Pilate. In the drama that occurred in the receiving room of the jail, Milkman saw her transform herself from a tall woman to a short one. She convinced the jailer that the stolen bag of bones was only her dead husband. Of course, Pilate never married, but as she lied, her metamorphosis continued with her large eyes becoming small. It was not until Milkman and Guitar were released that she returned to her normal appearance. Pilate's ability to transform herself could have been superb acting only, but her other uncanny feats cause one to accept in her powers of metamorphosis.

This use of magic affirms Pilate's love for Milkman, for she still considered him to be the medium of continuity in her family's history. Long before this incident, Milkman had discovered, upon his first remembered meeting with Pilate, when he was twelve, that all the spellbinding stories which he had heard about her were true. Drawn to the exotic attraction of these stories, he visited her and "found her on the front steps sitting wide-legged in a long-sleeved, long-skirted black dress.... She was all angles, he remembered later, knees, mostly, and elbows. One foot pointed east and one pointed west" (36). The witchlike description suggests Pilate's capability for magic. Milkman's instinctive submission to her gives her power to guide his search, a search already established by Morrison as a quest for self identity. The symbolism of Pilate's pointing feet indicating both east and west places Pilate at the center, the matrix to which she draws those who need her guidance. This meeting with Milkman suggests further mythic content with Pilate, wily and Protean, and like Proteus "never discloses even to the skillful questioner the whole content of his wisdom. He will reply only to the question put to him, and what he discloses will be great or trivial, according to the question asked" (Joseph Campbell, *The Hero With a Thousand Faces*, p. 381).

Morrison demonstrated this characteristic in Pilate's short answers to the questions posed by Milkman and Guitar. She cleverly put Milkman on the defensive about his name and proceeded to talk of small things. Her effect on him was narcotic and it is through this "pleasant semi-stupor" that Milkman listened to Pilate's story of her past. Her revelations indicate her divinization of her mother which is symbolized by her observing the color of the sky and the sacredness of her real name. "Same color as my Mama's ribbons. I'd know her ribbon color anywhere, but I don't know her name. After she died Papa wouldn't let anybody say it" (42-43). In the tradition of myth, gods and goddesses are not called by real names. This clue combines with the unknown name of the first Macon Dead to form the spiritual source of the microcosm to which Pilate draws Milkman. She is the personification of its Center, the axis mundi, or the World Navel defined by Campbell as "the symbol of the continuous creation: the mystery of the maintenance of the world through the continuous miracle of vivification which wells within all things" (41). Campbell's definition is a convenient paradigm for analyzing Pilate who has no navel, but is herself the "umbilical point" through which Milkman will define his personal cosmos. Whoever comes under her influence "is imitating the deed of the original hero. His aim is to rehearse the universal pattern as a means of evoking within himself the recollection of the life-centering, life-renewing form" (43).

Earlier I referred to Solomon, Milkman's archetypal ancestor as a totem figure and hence the original hero. His legendary flight at Solomon's Leap is imitated by those who are touched by Pilate's power. Milkman's heroic quest stirs within him the memory of his own center. Consequently, he wanders inexorably to Solomon's Leap where he makes the inevitable jump which transcends time and space.

Another character who reveals a facet of Pilate's character, different in its meaning, is Circe, the black maid of the wealthy landowner who murdered Pilate's father. When Milkman visited Circe, he heard her version of the origin of his father and Pilate. From the beginning of this introduction to Circe, Morrison reveals her as a surrogate mother for Pilate which stems not only from her role as midwife at her birth, but also from her uncanny, paradoxical qualities which render her suitable for this role, for like Pilate, she has attributes of the Yoruban trickster-divinity Edshu sho "donned a hat that was on the one side red but on the other white, green before and black behind..." (Campbell, p. 45) and was consequently seen differently from nearly every angle. Campbell uses the folktale to illustrate the ubiquity of the World Navel. Milkman had experienced Pilate's ubiquity: Her uncanny ability to hear those who approached her house long before anyone else became aware of them; her immediate appearance at the jail to rescue him; and the magnetism with which she drew people to her. His father's reference to her as a snake is but another aspect of her trickster art. Thus when Milkman faced Circe, he saw, as he had seen in Pilate, a set of contradictory elements which frightened and attracted him. Circe's youthful voice seemed incompatible with her withered face while her general cultivated demeanor ("dainty habits") contrasted sharply with her tattered and soiled clothing. Pilate's voice was also beautiful and her clothing dirty. The setting in a rotting, once substantial house, the cobwebs and weimaraner dogs all added to the images surrounding Circe which evoked a mood of eerieness. Similarly, images related to Pilate were often "offbeat." Examples are snake, lizard, hoot owl, and rocks. Pilate's piny-winy smell was narcotic and produced a stupor in Milkman not unlike that effected by Circe's ginger root which was "pleasant, clean, seductive" (239).

Circe is obviously an analogue of Circe, the Greek godess who directed Odysseus to his home. Milkman received advice from Circe on how to reach the cave where his father's bones lay. She, herself, living out a curse on her white masters, exulted in the crumbling, rotting house with its expensive contents smashed to pieces by thirty weimaraners. "Never. Nothing. Not a speck of dust, not a grain of dirt, will I move. Everything in this world they lived for will crumble and rot" (247). Her resolution and its implementation are the only defenses which she has against the years of remembered greed and murder. Her one selfish wish was that, upon her own death, someone would find her body before it is devoured by the dogs. The most significant thing for Milkman, however touched he was by Circe's circumstances, and notwithstanding his offer to remove her from them, was the information which Circe gave him concerning his ancestors. This, combined with the directions to the cave, pointed him to the final stage of his search.

Circe, consequently, filled in the gaps of the story which Pilate could not give. Their combined stories complete the enigma of his origin except for the final clues in the song which the children of Shalimar sang in their play. Some irony can be seen in such clues resting with the very young, those much younger than Milkman. Yet without Pilate and Circe, the ballad itself would yield little meaning. Together they hold the key to Milkman's finding himself and his universe.

Pilate, then, functions as an extension or ativar of Circe while Circe, herself, is unquestionably the archetypal Queen Goddess of the world who is encountered by Milkman after he has followed Pilate's clues. She is "the bliss-bestowing goal of every hero's earthly and unearthly quest...the soul's assurance that, at the conclusion of its exile in a world of organized inadequacies, the bliss that was once known will be known again" (Campbell, p. 111). The paradoxical charm of Circe suggests the qualities of the Universal Goddess, and Milkman, repeating his submission to Pilate, could not resist her. "...he followed her--his arm outstretched, his hand in hers--like a small boy being dragged reluctantly to bed" (240). Consistent with Campbell's explanation of the meeting with the goddess, Milkman's meeting with Circe becomes the revelation which is needed for the completion of his journey. The unanimity of qualities possessed by Pilate and Circe evokes the fanciful question of whether they are one person in the context of Pilate's conjurative power and her ubiquity. Logically, of course, this is a farfetched idea and perhaps of no service in establishing Pilate's character. It does exemplify Morrison's ability to stir the imagination, and the flights into dark passages of the mind to which her characterization of Pilate transports the reader.

Through Macon, Ruth, Milkman, and Circe, Morrison reveals the facets of Pilate's character which demonstrate her complexity. The ambiguity with which her characterization is embued is skillfully maintained and it correlates very well with the idea of Pilate as conjuress. No complete, clear delineation of character would be consistent with Morrison's obvious intent to have Pilate serve as a supernatural force around which the other characters move. She is the most skillfully drawn character in the Morrison canon with the long, carefully sustained development woven through other characters whom she affected. Pilate, the conjure woman, will long evoke fresh insights into her unfathomable, inscrutable personality.

QUESTIONS

1. The conjuror is a familiar figure in much of the fiction by American blacks. Compare and contrast Morrison's handling of Pilate with the conjuror in a work by Charles W. Chesnutt, Zora Neale Hurston, Ernest J. Gaines or any other black fiction writer.

2. Determine the extent to which Pilate's character is necessary in Milkman's development. For example, could Milkman have achieved self knowledge through another medium?

3. In the two households, that of Macon Dead and that of Pilate, which would you label sterile and which one is rich - by your standards and by the standards of society?

4. Under what conditions does Morrison embue Pilate with unselfish love and generosity?

5. Show how Morrison establishes the importance of family history in her treatment of Pilate.

6

Pilate Dead: A Symbol Of The Creative Imagination

> ...I come
> To answer thy best pleasure: be't to fly
> To swim, to dive into the fire, to ride
> on the cure'd clouds.
>
> Shakespeare, *The Tempest*,
> I, ii, ll. 99-102.

At once both strange and fascinating, Pilate Dead is the most singular creation in Toni Morrison's gallery of portraits. Pilate, a guileless and uninhibited soul, unobtrusively weaves a spell over those about her and controls the narrative fabric of *Song of Solomon*. In dispensing her magic and charm, Pilate exhibits wizardry, ingenuity and inventiveness as well as a sense of history and moral vision, elements in the creative process. In so doing, she becomes symbolic of the novelist's creative imagination.

That Pilate Dead is a wizard is reflected in the aura of mystery that surrounded her birth. She "borned herself." Through a strange twist of circumstances she was born without a navel "with a belly that looked like a back." Circe, the attending midwife, commented, "I had very little to do with it. I thought they were both dead, the mother and child. When she popped out, you could have knocked me over. I hadn't heard a heartbeat anywhere. She just came out" (244). In "borning" herself, Pilate became the "maker" or "creator" in the sense in which the Ancients spoke of the poet represented in the Greek work "poiein." As a "maker" or "creator," Pilate had supernatural powers, a distinction that set her apart. She possessed that intuitiveness, the proverbial sixth sense, or, more specifically, what Wordsworth refers to as "more than usual organic sensibility." In endowing Pilate with supernaturalness from birth, Morrison was able to create a more willing suspension of disbelief in her treatment of the character.

Pilate was as much at home in the supernatural world as in the natural world. She took her inspiration from and often listened "to her mentor — the father who appeared before her sometimes and told her things" (150).

Pilate was sixteen when she knew that she was different. Recognizing that her stomach was as "blind as a knee," she began to feel the ostracism of the men and hear the unkind whispers of the women. And though she was "hampered by huge ignorances, but not in any way unintelligent," Pilate began to accommodate herself to "what situation in the world was and would probably always be," and she "threw away every assumption she had learned and began at zero" (149). Pilate took an existentialistic view of her situation and asserted her creativity and began to carve out her own niche in the world: "Throughout this fresh, if common pursuit of knowledge, one conviction crowned her efforts: since death held no terrors for her (she spoke often to the dead), she knew there was nothing to fear" (149). Pilate began to ask herself the same questions that the creative artist asks: "When am I happy and when am I sad and what is the difference? What do I need to know to stay alive? What is true in the world? Her mind traveled crooked streets and aimless goat paths, arriving sometimes at profundity, other times at the revelations of a three-year old" (149). Pilate set out to find the truth, a requisite lauded by Plato as the ultimate goal of creative art. Pilate sought the reasons why and the answers to life's perplexing questions. She took risks in the same way that the creative artist does and according to Lawrence Ferlinghetti constantly risks "absurdity/and death/whenever he performs/above the heads of his audience." In proceeding fearlessly into the unknown, Pilate's creative spirit asserted itself. Pilate not only played by ear, she played by all of her other senses, and above all, she played by that extra sensibility that all creative artists possess. In the final analysis, Pilate, "whose equilibrium overshadowed all her eccentricities" (139) always struck a balance.

Pilate's creativity and ingenuity can also be seen in her ability to charm, to cast entrancing spells. Her brother Macon warned Milkman, "She's a snake and can charm like a snake, but still a snake" (54). Indeed, Pilate did charm. She cast a spell over Macon and induced him to impregnate Ruth in spite of his contempt for both Pilate and Ruth. But Macon came out of his "sexual hypnosis in a rage and later when he discovered her pregnancy, tried to get her to abort" (131). Pilate came to Ruth's rescue and worked her magic again. This time Pilate used black magic:

> (Years later Ruth learned that Pilate put a small doll on Macon's chair in his office. A male doll with a small painted chicken bone stuck between its legs and a round red circle painted on its belly. Macon knocked it out of the chair and with a yardstick pushed it into the bathroom, where he doused it with alcohol and burned it. It took nine separate burnings before the fire got down to the straw and cotton ticking of its insides. But he must have remembered the round fire-red stomach, for he left Ruth alone after that.) (132)

Pilate hypnotized and entranced through her singing. Her singing first attracted the attention of the people gathered to watch Robert Smith in his suicide jump from the top of Mercy Hospital. Later, even Macon was pulled "like a carpet tack under the influence of a magnet" (28) to her Spartan-like dwelling where he listened to Pilate, Reba and Hagar sing:

> Near the window, hidden by the dark, he felt the irritability of the day drain down from him and realised the effortless beauty of the women singing in the candlelighted... Singing now, her [Pilate's] face would be a mask; all emotion and passion would have left her features and entered her voice....
> As Macon felt himself softening under the weight of memory and music, the song died down. The air was quiet and yet Macon Dead could not leave. He liked looking at them freely this way. They didn't move. They simply

>stopped singing and Reba went on paring her toenails, Hagar threaded and unthreaded her hair, and Pilate swayed like a willow over her stirring. (29)

Even before Milkman met Pilate, the stories that he had heard about her had him spellbound. When Guitar and Milkman first visited Pilate and got a chance to enter her house, her "pebbly voice, the sun, and the narcotic wine smell weakened both the boys, and they sat in a pleasant semi-stupor, listening to her go on and on..." (40). Milkman found Pilate different from the stories that he had heard about her. He enjoyed going to Pilate's house with Guitar. He also enjoyed his new found cousins, Reba and Hagar, her daughter. Pilate's eccentricities both fascinated and hypnotized Milkman, but they also evoked complete happiness and trust.

Pilate also possessed a sense of history, a sense of tradition, a consciousness regarding the past, which both Lionel Trilling and T. S. Eliot extol as requisite to creativity. With Pilate, the past was not dead, but was inspiration for the present. Though she sometimes did not understand it, she never denied the past, never obliterated it from her thoughts. The haunting ballad that she sang throughout the novel immediately brings the past into focus:

> "O Sugarman done fly away
> Sugarman done gone
> Sugarman cut across the sky
> Sugarman gone home...."
> (6)

But Pilate's song was not simply about an African who flew back home, but, more importantly, it was about who she was and where she came from. In a word, Pilate sang about her roots. When her father's spirit leaned in at the window and said, "You just can't fly off and leave a body" (147), Pilate made her pilgrimage back to Danville, Pennsylvania, to pick up her "inheritance" which she shouldered from then until death in the same way that Christian in Bunyan's *The*

Pilgrim's Progress shouldered his burden of sin. But though Pilate thought that she had been shouldering her own burden of guilt, the bones of the white man that she and Macon had killed in the cave many years earlier, she actually had been carrying the bones of her dead father. When Milkman retraced Pilate's journey, he was able to fathom the mystery of the bones. He exclaimed,

> "Pilate! He didn't mean that. He wasn't talking about the man in the cave. Pilate! He was talking about himself. His own father flew away. He was the 'body.' The body you couldn't fly off and leave.... Pilate, your father's body floated up out of the grave you all dug for him. ONe month later it floated up. The Butlers, somebody, put his body in the cave... That was your father you found. You've been carrying your father's bones.. all this time." (333)

Pilate's naive response was a simple question: "Papa... I've been carrying Papa" (333)? In their last pilgrimage to Shalimar, Virginia, their ancestral home, Pilate and Milkman dug a grave on the top of Solomon's Leap not far from Ryna's Gulch and laid her father's bones to rest in the place where they belonged. At that instant, she was felled by a shot fired by Guitar. It was as if she had come full circle to the appointed time and place for her own death.

Finally, Pilate possessed moral vision which Matthew Arnold refers to as high seriousness. Pilate's life extended far beyond the narrow bounds of the here and the now, far beyond herself and her immediate environment. Early in life she developed a deep concern for human relationships. She loved much. Notwithstanding Macon's contempt for her, Pilate continued to love him. Her last words to Milkman sum up her philosophy of life: "Watch Reba for me... I wish I'd knowed more people. I would of love 'em all. If I'd a knowed more, I would a loved more" (336). Pilate's last words are a profound understatement. If she had possessed greater knowledge, she would have had a greater capacity for love. How ironical! Could

Pilate have loved more? It is doubtful. Intuitively, Pilate accepted the command of Christ to, "love one another, even as I have loved you, love ye one another," and she exhibited her love to the extent of self-denial. A peacemaker, Pilate was one of those of whom Christ said, "They shall be called the children of God." Most of all she epitomized the words of the prophet Micah who said, "He hath showed thee, O man, what is good; and what doth the Lord require of thee, but to do justly, and to love mercy, and to walk humbly with thy God?"

"Who knows what Pilate knows?" asked Macon Dead.

"Only the Shadow knows," Milkman replied.

Indeed, only the Shadow knows what mysteries of life, death, and eternity were housed in her soul. Musician, priestess, magician, folk historian, prophetess — Pilate epitomized the creative imagination.

QUESTIONS

1. Discuss what you consider to be important elements of the creative process.

2. Discuss Pilate Dead as a creator.

3. Discuss some of the risks involved in the creative process.

4. What are some of the common concerns of Pilate and Milkman?

5. Does the aura of mystery about Pilate ever subside? Discuss.

6. Compare Pilate as a creative force with a poet or musician whom you know.

7 ANARCHY IN SONG OF SOLOMON

The novels of Toni Morrison treat anarchistic tendencies, spawned by degrading experiences of various kinds, which propel some characters to rebellion against the prevailing ethical system. These experiences provide a rationale for many of the bizarre elements employed by Morrison. Yet, she does not concern herself with exposition on socio-political theory in her treatment of anarchy. Instead, she allows the experiences of her characters to provide the inferences for choices made by those who are in flight from or rebellion against the established order of their milieu.

Racial injustice, an uncontested given in her first three novels, is the underlying force in *Song of Solomon* from which the anarchistic tendencies of Guitar Bains and Macon Dead evolve. The injustice inflicted by the ruling power is treated alongside the more personal victimizations which result in lawlessness. Whether the impelling force is more broadly social or immediately personal, the characters react, both rationally and irrationally, from an awareness, at some point, of their own power. Such awareness is accompanied by a paradoxical freedom to act against the ruling authority. Any design of action chosen by the victim is deemed by him to be right.

The first Macon Dead, a successful black landowner, residing in bliss with his family, was killed by his white neighbor who wanted his land. The murder was committed in the presence of the victim's two children who were indelibly stamped with the memory of the event. One of the children, the second Macon Dead, was catapulted by the memory to an unethical, exploitive life of greed. The Guitar Bains subplot provides an analogue to the anarchy spawned by the brutal murder of the first Macon Dead as he sat on his fence at his farm in Pennsylvania. Guitar, a friend of the murdered man's grandson, was the son of a man who was "...sliced up in a sawmill and his boss came by and gave us kids some candy. Divinity. A big sack of divinity. His wife made it special for us. It's sweet, divinity is. Sweeter than syrup. Real sweet. Sweeter than..." (61). Since that time an anathema for sweets was retained by Guitar, who often vomited while thinking of them. Yet his anarchy was the result of something else. "It wasn't the divinity from the foreman's wife that made him sick. That came later. It was the fact that instead of life insurance, the sawmill owner gave his mother forty dollars 'to tide you and the kids over,' and she took it happily and bought each of them a big peppermint stick on the very day of the funeral. Guitar's two sisters and baby brother sucked away at the bone-white and blood-red stick, but Guitar couldn't" (224-225). This memory of his mother's gratitude for the forty dollars included her looking at the foreman with "a willingness to love." The pain inflicted by the whites, which forty dollars and sweets were supposed to assuage, was made unbearable by the acceptance and willingness of his mother. Degraded and permanently angered, Guitar was qualified by temperament to join the anarchists who called themselves The Seven Days and who avenged violent crimes committed by whites against blacks.

Morrison demonstrated the type of anarchy which is caused by racial injustice in *The Bluest Eye* in Cholly Breedlove's unhappy path of confusion and disorder, beginning when he was abandoned on a junk heap at the age of four days. Although he was rescued and reared by a great aunt, he received the compelling launch into an indelible hatred in adolescence when he was forced by two white men to have sexual intercourse with the young black girl with whom he was startled as they neared the end of their first sexual encounter. "With a violence born of helplessness," Cholly performed the act and directed his hatred, not to those who had humiliated him, but to the girl.

> His subconscious knew what his conscious mind did not guess — that hating them would have consumed him, burned him up like a piece of soft coal, leaving only flakes of ash and a question mark of smoke. He was, in time, to discover that hatred of white men — but not now. Not in

> impotence but later, when the hatred could find sweet expression. For now, he hated the one who had created the situation, the one who bore witness to his failure, his impotence. The one whom he had not been able to protect, to spare, to cover from the round moon glow of the flashlight. (118)

Cholly's hatred, therefore, was deflected to the girl who had caused him to be there and who had witnessed his debasement. Eventually, his anarchy, born of degradation, ran its chaotic course through joblessness, drunkenness and finally his assault of his daughter Pecola.

All of the foregoing instances of anarchy, spawned by racial debasement, illustrate the frustrations experienced by those who must impotently submit to the ruling power. Inherent in each experience is a need to break out of the confines of that power by any means available and to act freely on one's own power. For Macon Dead, Guitar and Cholly the personal power which is mustered is that which operates against convention. In addition, the compulsion to exert one's own power, to strike out, is far stronger than any moral or social system.

Circe, Milkman's guide in *Song of Solomon*, is further illustration of such compulsion which becomes a madness that creates its own rationality. The burden of her knowledge of her employer's heinous crime against the Dead family and the insensitivity to her labor festered throughout the remainder of her service to the Butler family. She spent an incredibly long old age, after they died, living out a prophecy or, more precisely, a curse. Her reflections were shared with the third Macon Dead, Milkman.

> They loved this place. Loved it. Brought pink veined marble from across the sea for it and hired men in Italy to do the chandelier that I had to climb a ladder and clean with white muslin once every two months. They loved it. Stole for it, lied for it, killed for it. But I'm the one left. Me and the dogs. And I will never clean it again. Never. Nothing. Not a speck of dust,

and the Seven Days. Common to both instances of anarchy is an awareness, at some point, of the helplessness that only increases with passivity. Acting instinctively to exert power of any sort, lawless or lawful becomes essential and is easily rationalized. The prevailing system has failed and is replaced in desperation.

The distraught Henry Porter, one of the Seven Days in *Song of Solomon*, cried

> Gimme hate, Lord... I'll take hate any day. But don't give me love. I can't take no more love, Lord. I can't carry it. Just like Mr. Smith. He couldn't carry it. It's too heavy. Jesus, you know. You know all about it. Ain't it heavy? Jesus? Ain't love heavy? Don't you see, Lord? Your own son couldn't carry it. If it killed Him, what You think it's gonna do to me? Huh? Huh? (26)

Thus Porter rationalizes his anarchy which he intends to bring to a spectacular close by killing himself. He had chosen hate, the dynamo of the Seven Days, but the intrusion of love — for those for whom he sought revenge, and the intrusion of frustration born of the loneliness of isolation, were too heavy a burden for him. This view is substantiated by Porter's "recovery" after his meeting and courtship of First Corinthians, Milkman's sister.

A similar pattern of rationalization is seen in the frequent conversations carried on in Tommy's Barbershop, the hub for members of the Seven Days and other black men whose opinions "crisscross" against the rhythm of the black idiom. Milkman and Guitar encountered the owners of the barbershop, Hospital Tommy and Railroad Tommy, as boys and learned how they thought on various subjects. An important speech in the novel is one given by Railroad Tommy to teach the boys the omnipresence of negation in their lives. He catalogued many desirable experiences and things which will be denied the boys and concluded, "Well, now. That's something you will have--a broken heart...And folly. A whole lot of folly. You can count on it" (61). This dadaistic account of the absurdity of expectations for the young is an important introduction to the irrationality of a world which needs the Seven Days. As the older men, most of them members of the Days, discussed the murder of Emmett Till, the rationale is presented in the heat of discussion by Hospital Tommy, a voice of reason. "I'm serious now...There is no cause for all this. The boy's dead. His mama's screaming. Won't let them bury him. That ought to be enough colored bloood on the streets. You want to spill blood, spill the crackers' blood that bashed his face in" (81). Hospital Tommy takes the approach that reason dictates that the one-sideness of black killings should be balanced by white killings. The syllogistic details are later supplied by Guitar as he defines for Milkman the mission of the Seven Days.

The argument of balance is introduced by Guitar in defining the Seven Days.

> I suppose you know that white people kill black people from time to time, and most folks shake their heads and say, "Eh, eh, eh, ain't that a shame?... I can't suck my teeth and say 'Eh, eh, eh.' I had to do something. And the only thing left to do is balance it; keep things on an even keel. Any man, any woman, or any child is good for five to seven generations of heirs before they're bred out. So even death is the death of five to seven generations. You can't stop them from killing us, from trying to get rid of us. And each time they succeed, they get rid of five to seven generations. I help keep the numbers the same. (154)

Guitar's rationale admits that no amount of counterviolence will stop whites from killing blacks. Yet balance is important because it is the only thing left. Furthermore, anarchy abhors passivity, and any action is better than none at all. With its mathematical symmetry, balance is its own excuse although it is a perverse form whose "sweetness" is not obviated by the matter of innocent people as its victims. "So you just get any one of them. There are no innocent white people, because every one of them is a potential nigger-killer, if not an actual one. You think Hitler surprised them? You think just because they went to war they thought he was a freak? Hilter's the most natural white man in the world. He killed Jews and Gypsies because he didn't have us" (155). Guitar infers, further, that the natural prey of white men is the black man. When the "right" prey is unavailable, as with Hitler, an appropriate substitution is made. Hence, he reasons, to say that whites who commit atrocities against blacks are crazy or ignorant is not enough. "That's like saying they were drunk. Or constipated...how come Negroes...don't get that crazy and that ignorant? No. White people are unnatural...and it takes a strong effort of the will to overcome an unnatural enemy" (156). A new dimension of the kind of anarchy exercised by the Seven Days is given here. The "strong effort of the will" alludes to a volition aligned with a specifically directed intention to act. Here Guitar supplies the chief requisite for membership which could not be sustained by many persons. One such person was possibly Freddie, an employee of Macon Dead. Morrison does not specifically identify Freddie as one of the Days, but his knowledge of them, their antagonism towards him imply that he was once one of them. He was berated for cowardice by Henry Porter and in his actions he displays a weakness which could belie any trust. He did not fit the rationale as perceived by Guitar.

Guitar defends his "reasonableness" by dismissing any aims of acting for fun, power or out of anger.

> Not at all. I hate doing it. It's hard to do it when you aren't angry or drunk or doped up or don't have a personal grudge against the person...I told you. Numbers. Balance. Ratio. And the earth, the land...The earth is soggy with black people's blood. And before us Indian blood... if it keeps on there won't be any of us left and there won't be any land for those who are left. So the numbers have to remain static. (157)

In the universe of *Song of Solomon* the loss of land is epitomized by the first Macon Dead's unsuccessful attempt to keep his farm. His murder was accompanied by the usurpation of his land which he had refused to relinquish to whites. Guitar equates every life taken with the taking of land from those left behind.

Finally, Guitar upholds the superiority of the Seven Days over the Mafia and the Klan who kill "for money and for fun." Milkman, throughout the argument, remains unconvinced that there is justification for the existence of the Seven Days. "There's too much wrong with it...you'll get caught eventually." Guitar then adds the motive of integrity to his anarchy. "Maybe. But if I'm caught I'll just die earlier than I'm supposed to. And how I die or when doesn't interest me. What I die for does" (159). To Milkman's claim that there is no love in it, Guitar supplies the rejoinder that "What I'm doing ain't about hating white people. It's about loving us. About loving you. My whole life is love" (159). He seems unaware of what that "love" did to Porter. This transposition of what was obvious hatred to Milkman into love can be related to the strong effort of the will required of the Seven Days. An acceptance of the rationale required this. Guitar finally informs him that because of the work of the Seven Days whites would one day think before they lynch. Since nihilism is the only thing Milkman saw in Guitar's revelation, the argument ended with both young men, with great irony, expressing fear for each other.

Thus balance for the Seven Days represents an immovable truth which is as unshakable as a mathematical theorem and as coldly rational. One must "see" the equation and have the will and courage to execute it. Guitar saw the denials or negations as defined by Railroad Tommy. His anarchy is causal and perhaps necessary while it maintains a natural reflexive quality that takes it out of the realm of the utter perverseness of atrocities committed by whites in the novel. At the same time Guitar shows himself to be sensitive and ethical in his remorse for, years after the incident, the accidental shooting of a doe during a boyhood hunting expedition. That this kind of sensitivity could exist alongside the mission of the Seven Days is an irony which Morrison has utilized perhaps to emphasize the complexity of motivation on the part of those who join the Days. Adherence to the law of the hunt, similar to the situation in Faulkner's "The Bear," is mandatory. A disciplined hunter would never violate that law, and the dedication required of the Days was no less mandatory. Immature judgment, rashness, and cowardice characterize the person who violates either set of laws. Integrity, required by both, marks the immovable path of manly expedition. Such was the view that Guitar had of his mission.

The attainment of this integrity involves knowing oneself. Morrison's technique in developing the heroic quest of Milkman revolves around the stages of his attainment of self knowledge. His friend Guitar knew who he was. "Guitar is my name. Bains is the slave master's name. And I'm all of that. Slave names don't bother me; but slave status does" (160). This identification of self gave him a stance from which to act. Milkman was still seeking his own identity and his search led him to Solomon's Leap where, with ambiguous finality, he "flew" towards Guitar in a terrifying leap of recognition.

Anarchy in Morrison's works reflects the frustrations of her characters and provides a vehicle for much of the grotesque which characterizes the novels. These categories of the grotesque which have been treated in an earlier chapter intensify the actions. Anarchy, as Morrison defines it, requires a perception of the futility of existence in the established order and the will to act. Anarchistic action itself requires creating one's own authority or rules, and in each case with Morrison's characters, complete freedom is enjoyed in the restructuring of lives that are made bearable by the change. Morrison explicitly wrote in *Sula* that some of her characters improvised life as they experienced it. They are experimenters searching for a new order in which they can believe. The import of depicting anarchy of several types is not an academic, socio-political statement, but an illustrated, reflective statement on the effect that a society has on individuals to whom the established order is hostile or indifferent. The resulting sense of debasement breeds the forms of revolt to which Macon Dead, Guitar and Circe turned.

QUESTIONS

1. Under what circumstances does Toni Morrison elicit sympathy for characters who are anarchistic?

2. Discuss whether any rationale can justify anarchy.

3. Indicate whether alternative actions would have served Morrison's anarchists as effectively as their chosen modes of conduct.

4. In viewing the character, Circe, does the reader receive an implied warning that long silence in the face of wrong is devastating to the individual? Explain your answer.

5. Do you consider Guitar or society responsible for the kind of man which he became?

8
GREEK TRAGIC MOTIFS IN SONG OF SONG OF SOLOMON

Toni Morrison's *Song of Solomon* follows a darkly tragic pattern that is strikingly similar to Greek tragedy. Although Morrison's novel would not fit the strict design of Greek tragedy as codified by Aristotle, tragic motifs are apparent from the outset as she recounts the story of the House of Dead, as it were, whose lives appear to be dominated by the inevitable doom of a family curse, ancestral guilt and incestuous relations. In addition, Morrison adroitly includes other motifs such as the chorus and the achieving of an epiphany. Morrison intermingles these elements of Greek tragedy and the black American experience as she relates the story of a young black man's search for his roots.

The ancestral history of the House of Dead is embedded in the words of the haunting ballad that sets the darkly tragic mood of the novel:

> "O Sugarman done fly away
> Sugarman done gone
> Sugarman cut cross the sky
> Sugarman gone home...."
> (6)

The story is, in fact, the song of Shalimar, later corrupted to Solomon, Shalimar, Virginia, being the ancestral home of the House of Dead and Sugarman being the progenitor of the family. Sugarman, transported to America as an African slave, "Just stood up in the fields one day, ran up some hill, spun around a couple of times, and was lifted up in the air. Went right on back to wherever it was he came from" (323).

From the very outset, the House of Dead was apparently overshadowed by the inevitable doom of the curse associated with Sugarman's flight. In his escape, Sugarman had attempted to take his son Jake under his arm, but during the flight Jake fell. Sugarman continued his flight, but Jake was rescued by

Heddy, an Indian woman. Sugarman's wife, Ryna, lost her mind and pined away and her name was given to Rynah's Gulch, a pining ghost-ridden ravine. Jake's wife, Sing, died during the birth of Pilate, her baby girl, born without a navel with "a belly that looked like a back" and "as blind as a knee." Their son, Macon, married Ruth Foster who possessed an electra complex. Macon and Ruth's son was forced into an uncanny relationship with Ruth suggesting an oedipus complex. The family lived in a palatial house behind the facade of which lay a spiritual mortuary and psychological prison. In brief, it appears that the characters in the novel are subjected to an evil for which they are in no way responsible.

The family also appears to be entrapped or cursed by the surname "Dead," a name in which doom is implicit. One wonders why Jake, who was given the name Macon Dead, never bothered to change the surname "Dead." It rather appears that Jake took it as a part of his destiny. Likewise, his son Macon felt the entrapment of the name:

> Surely, he thought, he and his sister had some ancestor, some lithe young man with onyx skin and legs as straight as cane stalks, who had a name that was real. A name given to him at birth with love and seriousness. A name that was not a joke, nor a disguise, nor a brand name... His own parents in some mood of perverseness or resignation, had agreed to abide by a naming done to them by somebody who couldn't have cared less. Agreed to take and pass on to all their issue this heavy name scrawled in perfect thoughtlessness by a drunken Yankee in the Union Army. A literal slip of the pen handed to his father on a piece of paper and which he handed to his only son, and his son likewise handed on to his; Macon Dead who begat a second Macon Dead who married Ruth Foster (Dead) and began Magdalene called Lena Dead and First Corinthians Dead and (when he least expected it) another Macon Dead, now known to the part of the world that mattered as Milkman Dead. And as if that were not enough, a sister called Pilate Dead. (17-18)

The name became an albatross for the family and especially for the third Macon Dead called Milkman who approximates the tragic hero of Greek drama. Milkman resented the fact that his grandfather, Jake, who became the first Macon Dead "took" that name: "'Somebody should have shot him.'" His friend, Guitar, retorted, "'What for? He was already dead'" (89). The irony implicit in Guitar's comment suggests that doom surrounded the family by virtue of its surname. When Milkman first met his aunt, Pilate, his resentment for the name became a defense. When Pilate told Milkman, "'Ain't but three Deads alive,'" Milkman responded defensively, "'I'm a Dead! My mother's a Dead! My sisters. You and him ain't the only ones'" (38). Milkman felt that the name would also be an encumbrance if he studied medicine as his mother so much desired and he asked her, "'How would that look? M. D., M.D. If you were sick would you go see a man called Dr. Dead'" (69)?

The name "Milkman" also gave the third Macon Dead serious cause for concern, and he felt that it, too, was an albatross. He nor his father ever knew exactly why he was given the nickname, but both felt that it was because of something unsavory. The doom surrounding the nickname is suggested by Guitar's comment: "'The cards are stacked against us and just trying to stay in the games, stay alive and in the game, makes us do funny things'" (87). Guitar concluded: "'Let me tell you somethin, baby. Niggers get their names the way they get everything else — the best way they can. The best way they can'" (89).

In addition to a nickname and a surname that appear ill-fated, Milkman also had a deformity:

> By the time Milkman was fourteen he noticed that one of his legs was shorter than the other. When he stood barefoot and straight as a pole, his left foot was about an inch off the floor. So he never stood straight; he slouched or leaned or stood with a hip thrown out, and he never told anybody about it — ever. (62)

Ironically, what was an imperfection became a heroic quality for Milkman because he felt a secret connection with President Franklin D. Roosevelt. It also made him a hero with the girls because he danced with a "curious stiff-legged step that the girls loved and other boys eventually copied" (62). This deformity may also be compared with Oedipus' swollen ankle in Greek drama.

Milkman's supernatural powers are also evident. He was always just a hairbreadth away from death, but somehow he always managed to escape death. Even before he was born, his father tried to make his mother abort him. Ice-pick wielding Hagar tried many times to kill him. He felt that Circe also tried to kill him. He encountered bats in a cave and managed to escape them. And when he reached his ancestral home, Shalimar, Virginia, "he walked into a store and asked if somebody could fix his car and a nigger pulled a knife on him. And he still wasn't dead" (270).

Ironically, Milkman received a hero's welcome in Danville, but when he reached Shalimar things were different: "In his own home town his name spelled dread and grudging respect. But here, in his 'home,' he was unknown, unloved, and damn near killed. These were some of the meanest unhung niggers in the world" (270). Milkman's situation in his ancestral "home" maybe compared with the situation with which Christ was confronted in his hometown when He asserted in Matthew 13:57, "A prophet is not without honor, save in his own country, and in his own house."

The Greek tragic models frequently involved incestuous relationships. To a degree, such is also the case in *Song of Solomon*. Ruth Foster's relationship with her father, the town's only black doctor, before and after her marriage to Macon Dead gave the appearance of incest if indeed no actual sexual intimacy ever occurred. She kissed him goodnight on his lips up to the time that she was sixteen and married Macon. Dr. Foster delivered both of Ruth's daughters, Magdalene called Lena and First Corinthians, a fact that Macon found revolting. Immediately after Dr. Foster's death, Macon discovered Ruth with her father,

> "In the bed. That's where she was when I opened the door. Laying next to him. Naked as a yard dog, kissing him. Him dead and white and puffy and skinny, and she had his fingers in her mouth." (73)

Many years later when Milkman surreptitiously followed his mother on a midnight excursion and discovered that she had been going to the Fairfield Cemetery in Fairfield Heights to lie on her father's grave, he coolly and cruelly confronted her, and she explained that Dr. Foster, her father, was

> The only person who ever really cared whether I lived or died. Lots of people were interested in whether I lived or died, but he cared.... But he cared whether and he cared how I lived, and there was, and is, no one else in the world who ever did. And for that I would do anything. It was important for me to be in his presence, among his things, the things he used, had touched. Later it was just important for me to know that he was in the world. When he left it, I kept on reigniting that cared-for feeling that I got from him. (124)

Apparently, Ruth also received that cared-for feeling from Milkman when he was a little boy. Though Milkman was more victimized than guilty, he was a participant in what had all the rudiments of an incestuous relationship: Ruth would call

> ... her son to her. When he came into the little room she unbottoned her blouse and smiled. He was too young to be dazzled by her nipples, but he was old enough to be bored by the flat taste of mother's milk, so he came reluctantly, as to a chore, and lay as he had at least once each day of his life in his mother's arms, and tried to pull the thin, faintly sweet milk from her flesh without hurting her with his teeth. (13)

The daily occasions made Ruth's life bearable, but were to end when Freddie discovered them and called the boy, "'A milkman. That's what you got here, Miss Rufie. A natural milkman if ever I seen one. Lookout, womens. Here he come. Huh'" (15)! And thus the nickname, Milkman, came into being.

Closely related though not necessarily incestuous is Milkman's relationship with Hagar, the daughter of his first cousin, Reba. He met her when he was twelve and she was seventeen and they maintained an "off and on" relationship for the rest of her life. Milkman's relationship with Hagar was his initiation into manhood:

> Sleeping with Hagar had made him generous. Or so he thought. Widespirited. Or so he imagined. Widespirited and generous enough to defend his mother, whom he almost never thought about, and to deck his father, whom he both feared and loved. (69)

Incidentally, there is a symbolic relationship between Hagar and her biblical namesake who was Abraham's concubine. After a while, Hagar became "like the third beer" to Milkman, flat and boring. She retaliated by becoming Milkman's nemesis:

> As regularly as the new moon searched for the tide, Hagar looked for a weapon and then slipped out of her house and went to find the man for whom she believed she had been born into the world. Being five years older than he was and his cousin as well did nothing to dim her passion. In fact her maturity and blood kinship converted her passion to fever, so it was more affliction than affection. (127)

Community folk reacted negatively to the cousin-cousin relationship. A conversation in the beauty parlor exemplifies community feeling:

> "... I don't want no trouble with that girl Hagar. No telling what she might do. She jump that cousin of hers,

> no telling what she might do to me... Ought to be shamed, the two of them cousins." (312)

Pilate, of course, knew that Milkman's supernatural powers would save him from death at the hands of ice-pick wielding Hagar. She said: "Ain't nothin goin to kill him but his own ignorance, and won't no woman ever kill him" (140). The tragic mood is heightened by the death of Hagar. Her pathetic demise came at approximately the same time that Milkman embarked upon his new beginning.

As tragic hero, Milkman experienced a degree of catharsis, an epiphany, when he finally fitted together the pieces of the jigsaw puzzle regarding his ancestry. As he swam in the sea, undergoing a baptism, or purging, as it were, he pulled the entire puzzle together and exclaimed:

> "He could fly!... My great-granddaddy could fly!" He whipped the water with his fists, then jumped straight up as though he could take off, and landed on his back and sank down, his mouth and eyes full of water. Up again. Still pounding, leaping, diving... 'He didn't need no airplane... He could fly his own self." (329)

Milkman's revelation or new knowledge strengthened him and in the end he himself finally took what Kierkegaard refers to as the "leap of faith." Milkman "leaped" as he met Guitar willing to accept whatever fate awaited him. He, like Shalimar, his great-grandfather was willing to surrender to the air. Both knew that "If you surrendered to the air, you could ride it" (337).

Throughout the novel, Morrison makes use of the chorus in such a way that the reader becomes a part of the novel by virtue of being able to identify with the characters and events. Through the use of "community" information and lore such as folktales, folk expressions, proverbs, signs, omens, ghost stories, superstitions, and other folkisms, Morrison strikes a chord that is common among the readers. Each reader as well as the characters in the novel becomes a part of the chorus in the sense that the chorus is the omniscient and omnipotent force that moves the narrative along and comments on or gives assent to the action.

The haunting ballad that Pilate sang near the beginning of the novel which is also repeated throughout becomes the focal point around which the plot is built and sets the scene for all of the action. When Milkman heard the same melody and listened to the story told in the children's song as they played in the streets of Shalimar, Virginia, he began to realize that the song was indeed about him, his roots and his culture; and, thus, the song functions for the novel in the same way that Greek chorus commented on history of a family of high estate. In a sense, then, Pilate was a much a part of the chorus as the children of Shalimar, Virginia, whose song brought into focus the meaning of the words of Pilate's song:

> "O Sugarman done fly away
> Sugarman done gone
> Sugarman cut across the sky
> Sugarman gone home...."
>
> (6)

When Pilate first sang the melody, Robert Smith was attempting to fly from the top of Mercy Hospital to the other side of Lake Superior. He had written in a suicide note, "I will take off from Mercy and fly away on my own wings" (3). Pilate, already aware of her own ancestral history, was able to link the two events in a way that no other onlookers could. This becomes tragically ironic. Both Robert Smith and Sugarman were bound together in a way that was known only at first to Pilate, but in the final analysis, it is known by all of the characters. As the chorus, the chorus functioning also as a character in the novel which was a common feature of Greek literature, Pilate not only commented on the action, but participated in it likewise.

The omniscient and omnipresent position of the narrator allowed for frequent passages that set the stage for the action in the same way that the Greek chorus functioned. For instance, Chapter 10 opens with such a passage.

> When Hansel and Gretel stood in the forest and saw the house in the clearing before them, the little hairs at the nape of their necks must have shivered. Their knees must have felt so weak that blinding hunger alone could have propelled them forward. No one was there to warn them; their parents, chastened and grieving, were far away. So they ran as fast as they could to the house where a woman older than death lived, and they ignored the shivering nape hair and the softness of their knees. A grown man can also be energized by hunger, and any weakness in his knees or irregularity in his heartbeat will disappear if he thinks his hunger is about to be assuaged. Especially, if the object of his craving is not gingerbread or chewy gumdrops, but gold. (219)

Here, Morrison gives an insightful comment regarding different dimensions of hunger. It prepares the reader for the narration which follows regarding Milkman's quest for the gold. This and similar passages reflect that Morrison is attempting to produce the same effect that the Greek tragedians produced in their use of the chorus.

Scattered throughout the novel are other oblique allusions to Greek tragedy. One outstanding example is the character Circe who in Greek literature was an enchantress who turned men into swine as well as assisted Odysseus in his journey back to Ithaca. So, too, did Circe in *Song of Solomon*, who kept dogs, assist Milkman by guiding him on his journey to his ancestral home. Likewise, the journey that Milkman himself made to Shalimar, Virginia, parallels the idea of the heroic quest of Greek literature where the hero descends into the darkness of Hades before ascending to the heights of revelation and new knowledge.

In presenting a tragic view of life in *Song of Solomon*, Morrison did not woodenly design her narrative around Greek tragic motifs nor did she superimpose these motifs or her narrative. Rather, in a very unobtrusive way, Morrison presents the history of a family that unfolds tragically. Unlike Greek tragic models, however, Morrison's novel ends with the triumph of the hero over all adversity. Even if Guitar succeeds in killing Milkman, Milkman will remain triumphant because he nobly accepted the challenge to defend his position even at the risk of death.

QUESTIONS

1. Point out similarities between Milkman and Oedipus as tragic heroes.

2. How does ancestral guilt affect the lives of both Milkman and Oedipus?

3. What is significant about the relationship between Macon Dean and his sister, Pilate Dead?

4. Discuss the symbolic use of names in *Song of Solomon*.

5. Point out how the ballad that recurs throughout the novel serves to cement the separate parts of the narrative.

6. Point out some of the elements of folklore in the novel.

7. Discuss the biblical overtones found in the novel.

8. How is the theme of the quest sustained throughout the novel?

9. Garden Metaphor and Christian Symbolism in Tar Baby

Toni Morrison's *Tar Baby* is rich in metaphor and symbolism. Especially is there a strong relationship between the garden metaphor and Christian symbolism. Set in an exotic Caribbean island which "three hundred years ago struck slaves blind the moment they saw it" (8), Morrison's novel vividly depicts a terrestrial paradise where "trees mutter in their sleep," the "water-lady" cups you in the "palm of her hand" and "brushes your eyelids with her knuckles," "fog comes in wisps sometimes like the hair of maiden aunts," and "the whole island vomits up color." Her lush descriptions of such an exotic and picturesque landscape serve as the tapestry that forms the backdrop for a profound statement regarding the harsh realities of life.

The arcadian island with "hills and vales so beautiful it made visitors tired to look at them: bougainvillea, avocado, poinsettia, lime, banana, coconut and the last of the rain forest's champion trees " (10) may be compared with Milton's lines in *Paradise Lost* detailing the lushness of Eden:

> Yet higher than their tops
> The verdurous wall of Paradise up sprung:
> ....
> And higher than the Wall a circling row,
> Of goodliest Trees loaden with fairest Fruit,
> Blossoms and Fruits at once of golden hue
> Appear'd, with gay enamel'd colors mixt:
> On which the Sun more glad impress'd his beams
> Than in fair Evening cloud, or humid Bow
> When God hath show'r'd the

>   earth; so lovely seem'd
>   That Lantship.....
>   (Book IV, ll. 143-144, 146-153)

Like Milton, Morrison emphasizes the exotic beauty of the landscape. She exhibits a poetic flair for local color and the picturesque designed to engender a remoteness and beauty analogous to the Garden of Eden. But throughout this near paradise there are reminders of the Fall. Antagonistic features of nature reflect this fact. The narrator states:

> The end of the world, as it turned out, was nothing more than a collection of magnificent winter houses on Isle des Chevaliers. When laborers imported from Haiti came to clear the land, clouds and fish were convinced that the world was over, that the sea-green green of the sea and the sky-blue sky of the sky were no longer permanent. Wild parrots that had escaped the stones of hungry children in Queen of France agreed and raised havoc as they flew to look for yet another refuge. Only the champion daisy trees were serene. After all, they were part of a rain forest already two thousand years old and scheduled for eternity, so they ignored the men and continued to rock the diamondbacks that slept in their arms. It took the river to persuade them that indeed the world was altered.   (9)

This vivid description of how the world was altered may be compared with Milton's description of Eden after Eve plucked and ate the forbidden fruit:

>   Earth felt the wound, and Nature
>   from her seat
>   Sighing through all her Works gave
>   signs of woe,
>   That all was lost.
>   (Book IX, ll. 782-784)

As with Milton, Morrison asserts that nature reacted when mankind violated and abused her. With Milton, man's abuse was the great sin of commission in eating the forbidden fruit. With Morrison, man's abuse was not only the violation of nature in destroying the natural beauty and uprooting fowl and animals from their natural habitat; it was a violation of the rights of other men who were imported from Haiti as laborers as well as the slaves who were struck blind when they beheld the island. Thus it is that Morrison begins to juxtapose the prelapsarian and postlapsarian states of nature in an elaborate metaphor of the garden contrasting the beginning and the end of the world. Morrison overlaps these two layers of perspective throughout the novel. The ambivalently mixed landscape thus becomes symbolic of the ambivalent human condition that Morrsion depicts in the novel.

Valerian Street, a candy manufacturer, has retired to the idyllic Isle des Chevaliers. His young wife Margaret, the "Principal Beauty of Maine," has come with him unwillingly to what appears to her to be the equator, which itself becomes symbolic. Sydney and Nanadine Childs are the faithful servants who fulfill all of Valerian's needs and most of Margaret's. Their niece Jadine, a Sorbonne-educated dilettante, who has forgotten her "ancient properties" has come to the island for an extended vacation from her world of modelling, film and theater. These five live together in an outwardly peaceful and harmonious but inwardly highly antagonistic and potentially volatile household. In fact, the lives of these individuals are interwined with the mythic forces of nature that surround them. Just as nature had been altered, "evicted from the place where it had lived, and forced into unknown turf," so, too, have Margaret and the Childses been evicted from their natural habitats to come at Valerian's bidding to a land with which they are not in harmony. This fact appears to presage the conflict that is to come.

What has happened, however, is that somehow the Childses have assumed that they have been assimilated into the Street family. Especially does Jadine reflect this assumption in that she lives on the same "level" of the house that Margaret and Valerian do and she is even on a first name basis with them mistakenly believing that she is being accepted by them on that "level." To carry their assumption further, the Childses have absorbed the same patriarchal aloofness toward the island blacks as Margaret and Valerian exhibit. They refer to Gideon, the yardman, as "Yardman," and Nanadine speaks condescendingly to Therese, the blind laundry woman. When Son arrives on the scene, Sydney wastes no time is saying to him condescendingly: "I know you, but you don't know me. I am a Phil-a-delphia Negro mentioned in the book of the very same name. My people owned drugstores and taught school while yours were still cutting their faces open so as to be able to tell one of you from the other" (163). It is ironic that Sydney fails to recognize that on the island he is still no more than a hired servant, a butler, who still says "Yes, Sir," and "No, Sir to a man whom he must address as "Mr. Street." Herein lies the paradox. Sydney is attempting to revert to the ideal or the Golden Age, as it were, of his life in the past instead of accomodating himself to the reality of the present where, in fact, he now resides. Life indeed for him and his family was "altered" when they uprooted themselves. Sydney wants to enjoy life from both perspectives — past and present.

The dualities of the prelapsarian and postlapsarian states are projected further in the name of the impressively built house that the Streets and Childses occupy, L'Arbe de la Croix, which the narrator asserts is "an unfortunate choice of names." However, it is in the irony of the name that the symbolism lies. The house is both a garden and a cross symbolizinig at once the prelapsarian and postlapsarian state. Implicit in this paradox is also a suggestion regarding the occupants who live behind the facade of idyllic serenity but whose real existence is tortorous and whose lives exhibit signs of the Fall.

Recently added to L'Arbe de la Croix is the greenhouse, the domain of Valerian exclusively,

Margaret referring to it as a "shed." It is ironical that in an area as exotic and naturally beautiful as the Isle des Chevaliers Valerian would want a greenhouse simply to grow the hydrangea that he missed from not being in Philadelphia. It would appear that retirement to an exotic island in itself would be enough. But the very fact that Valerian spends most of his time on the island in the greenhouse drinking, reading, listening to his records and tending his plants leads us to another dimension of interpretation. The greenhouse, in fact, becomes symbolic of Valerian's attempt to recapture something that he has lost, and, more profoundly, it represents for Valerian a new beginning analogous to man's beginning. In essence, Valerian attempts to recreate the prelapsarian state: "The greenhouse made it possible to reproduce the hydrangea but the postman was lost to him forever" (11). Valerian worked hard to recapture that feeling of innocence represented in uncorrupted nature, the loss of which Wordsworth laments in "Ode on the Intimations of Immortality from Recollections of Early Childhood" when he says:

> But yet I know, where'er I go
> That there hath passed away a
> glory from the earth.

In his attempt to recreate the essence of unspoiled nature, Valerian spent most of his time in the greenhouse because "it was a nice place to talk to his ghosts in peace while he transplanted, fed, air-layered, rooted, watered, dried and thinned his plants" (14). His speaking to ghosts would further suggest that Valerian is attempting to recapture something that has vanished which reiterates the symbol of the greenhouse as representive of the prelapsarian state found in the Edenic setting of man's first paradise. Additionally, Valerian attempts to bring vitality to the greenhouse by playing his Goldberg variations of Chopin, Bach, Haydn, Liszt and Rampal, all of which nourish and sooth the plants in the tradition of the music of the spheres which Milton describes in "At a Solemn Music":

> Where the bright Seraphim in burning row
> Their loud uplifted angel-trumpets blow,
> And the Cherubic host in thousand choirs
> Touch their immortal Harps of golden wires,
> With those just Spirits that were victorious
>   Palms,
> Hymns devout and hold Psalms
> Singing everlasting;
> That we on Earth with undiscording voice
> May rightly answer that melodious noise;
> As once we did, till disproportion'd sin
> Jarr'd against nature's chime, and with
>   harsh din
> Broke the fair music that all
>   creatures made
> To their great Lord, whose love their
>   motion sway'd
> In perfect Diapason, whilst they stood
> In first obedience and their state
>   of good.
>   (ll. 10-24)

Implicit in these lines is the principle familiar in Milton's time that the Universe is one mighty, sweet-toned instrument acted on and guided by one Spirit. Then, perfect amity existed among all of its elements until "disproportion'd sin jarr'd against nature's chime." Likewise, Valerian uses music to help recreate the original harmony of the spheres for the rejuvenation, nourishment and protection of his plants in the greenhouse.

Related to the symbol of rejuvenation is the appearance of Son on the Isle de Chevaliers. The novel opens with his undergoing a ritualistic cleansing, a baptism, and new beginning, as it were, as he escapes his ship and swims through "blood-tinted water" to the island for asylum with only the clothes on his back and his shoes with their laces knotted through the belt hoop of his pants. Son's symbolic status in the novel takes on new meaning after he is discovered during the days leading up to Christmas. Having already undergone a new baptism, Son comes to L'Arbe de la Croix, the house that had a "hotel feel about it" and is invited to stay by the patriarchal "in-keeper," Valerian Street, which gives an ironic twist to the Christmas story. At this point, however, Son becomes an integral part of the Christian symbolism in the novel. Son, with "skin as dark as a riverbed, his eyes as steady and clear as a thief's" (113) is discovered in Margaret Street's closet as the occupants of the house are ostensibly preparing for the homecoming of the Streets' son Michael. An intruder in the otherwise placid and illusion-filled existence of these characters, Son becomes a Christian symbol, he himself representing at the same time one of the lonely, despised, rejected and downcast that Christ came to bring hope to and Christ himself. While it might seem inappropriate to say that Son as a character symbolizes Christ himself, one cannot deny the parallels that are found in the novel and the Christmas story. Too, Son reminds Valerian of Michael, his own son, the prodigal, as it were, who is expected home for Christmas. When Son appears, Valerian exchanges his "swaddling clothes" for a fine pair of silk pajamas and exchanges his "manger" for a guest room in the house, with Son becoming at once both the surprise guest and Valerian's surrogate son.

Most of all, Son's coming to L'Arbe de la Croix shatters the facade of harmony and pretense behind which the occupants of the house live in the same way that the birth of the infant Jesus shattered the hyprocrisies of that time. All of the pent up emotions and suppressed hostilities explode. All icons are dethroned and the shackles of hypocrisy crumble. This otherwise self-contained household realizes for the first time that they have been deluding themselves about who they really are and how they really relate to each other. Son brings truth, honesty, freedom and hope to the shallow lives of the occupants of L'Arbe de la Croix. As the person who emancipates the deluded householders, Son is suggestive of Christ's statement in St John 8:36 to the Jews who believed on Him: "If the Son therefore shall make you free, ye shall be free indeed."

The appellation Son, not unfamiliar in addressing young males in the black community, is also widely assumed as a given or Christian name by many vagrant black youths. Thus, William "Son" Green is not only the son of Franklin G. Green, called Old Man, but he in essence is a kind of universal son who is immediately identifiable by many people. Not only does Son remind Valerian of his own prodigal Michael, but Son himself is also a prodigal from his native Eloe, Florida, and when he returns, he is received with open arms by Old Man and his friends. His reunion with his own father is reminiscent of the reunion of the father and son in the parable that Jesus told, Son then becoming symbolic of the Son of Man and Son of God.

When Son shatters the illusions of the householders of L"Arbe de la Croix, the place becomes just what Margaret had called it when she first arrived on the island-- an "equator." It is at this point that all of the householders relate to each other as equals. Valerian and Margaret attempt to maintain their status as lord and mistress, but Sydney and Ondine rise to the occasion of their personhood. They stand eye to eye and shoulder to shoulder with Valerian and Margaret, asserting themselves as equals. Only Jadine is completed jaded, incapable of accepting what is actually happening. She has possibly been the most deluded one of all of them. Son's simple comment about what happens is "that white folks and black folks should not sit down and eat together ....They should work together sometimes, but they should not eat together or live together or sleep together. Do any of those personal things in life" (210). Son's comment, of course, is hyperbolic. Obviously eating together and sleeping together are more implicit references than explicit ones. What Son implies is that L'Arbe is a microcosm, a little world representative of the larger world. Participating in personal relationships cannot be accomplished even in a small world where disharmony exists. Son, being a product of a segregated society, speaks in terms of blacks and whites. But he could as easily have referred to any two groups of people who are divided by barriers of hypocrisy, sham, and pretension. Christ addressed the same concern in his words to the multitude when he said in St. Luke 12:1-2: "Beware ye of the leaven of the Pharisees, which is hypocrisy. For there is nothing covered, that shall not be revealed; neither hid, that shall not be known." What transpires at L'Arbe de la Croix reflects the harsh realities that prevent man's attainment of an earthly paradise, disharmony among men and nations resulting from the myriad hostilities that mar permanent relationships not only among men but also among nature. Until harmony is achieved among men and nations, paradise is only an elusive dream. Though an ideal devoutly to be wished, Eden is irretrievably lost to mortal man. Glimpses of Eden may be attained and mortals may intermittently enjoy its pleasures, but another Eden is a promise only for the truly redeemed. In a word, the new Eden is in the future, not in the past. Son's intrusion into the lives of the occupants of L'Arbe de la Croix symbolizes the beginning of regeneration and intensified the hope of redemption and the attainment of the new Eden. But it is now entirely up to each of the occupants to choose to accept or reject what Son embodies.

It is important to note that Son also brings the sun to the greenhouse. In a word, he is sun. The withered hydrangea bloomed. He "healed" the plant in a miraculous way just as he rid the greenhouse of the pesty ants by putting mirrors outside the greenhouse door: "They won't come near a mirror" (147). Valerian says to Margaret, "You should see the greenhouse now. Black magic" (189). Son's healing power underscores his status as a Christ symbol as well as his being symbolic of the sun which brings light and warmth to the plants. He does possess a kind of magic that saturates his environment. Son is "that certain kind of man" for whom "the mist lifted and the trees

5. Which character or characters symbolize the tar baby image?

6. Discuss the water imagery in the novel.

7. Discuss the relationship between the Streets and the Childses. Is it superficial? Hypocritical?

10   AN INTERVIEW WITH TONI MORRISON

This interview was taped on November 23, 1981, in Toni Morrison's office at Random House Publishers in New York. The questions represent the collaborative concerns of both Audrey Vinson and me. The reader recognizes each of our specific interests based on the essays which bear our signatures. The interview is the culmination of approximately a year and a half of intermittent correspondence between Miss Morrison and me. The transcript of the tape was edited by Miss Morrison and is published with her approval.

Jones: How do your own experiences growing up in Ohio compare with those in the novels? I suppose I am asking if you consider any of your novels as having autobiographical elements.

Morrison: It is difficult always for me and probably any writer to select those qualities that are genuinely autobiographical because part of what you are doing is re-doing the past as well as throwing it into relief, and what makes one write anyway is something in the past that is haunting, that is not explained or wasn't clear so that you are almost constantly rediscovering the past. I am geared toward the past, I think, because it is important to me; it is living history. I was very, very conscious of that mood and atmosphere of my hometown in the first book, *The Bluest Eye*, and used literal descriptions of neighborhoods and changed the obvious things, the names of people, and mixed things all up, but the description of the house where we lived, the description of the streets, the lake, and all of that, is very much the way I remember Lorain, Ohio, although people go there now and they don't see what I saw.

And more importantly, I seem to remember some people, at that time, (mind you this is with dazzling hindsight and also from the point of view of a child in which things are very much exaggerated and new and fresh) seemed mysterious to me and their mystery and their eccentricities were fascinating to me. And because we were unexamined at that time — Black people were unexamined and unstudied, at least it appeared so (laughter) to me, nobody was paying us too much attention in a scholarly sense. There were no social workers, you know, none of that, so what we did was unaffected and was not posed. There was enormous oppression but within that oppressive structure there was an incredible amount of freedom. That is reflected in *The Bluest Eye* and many of the others as well as my sense of not — even though I never lived in a Black neighborhood in Lorain, Ohio, because there weren't any, at that time — it was too small, too poor, to have officially racist structures. Our family's social life was very much confined to what we were doing but, you know, the schools, and stores and so on, and our next door neighbors were white people. There were always some on the block, or I guess they say there were always some of us on the block. So I grew up with Black and white children. However, and it's still astonishing to me, in spite of that proximity white people did not seem to appear very much in the life of the spirit or the mind. Which is a way of saying that there were two sorts of education that were going on — a school education, and another education, and the one that stuck was the one that was not in the school. Whatever my people said, that was the real life, subverted, I think, for a lot of my life when I left home. But you realize that whenever you get in a crisis situation that's where you go for help. So the philosophy is as accurate, the mood is as accurate as I can remember it, and some of it I don't remember. It is sort of like, I don't know, a racial recollection that I just have to trust even though I cannot claim to know it all. I did use my sister. I have an older sister, but our relationship was not at all like the girls in *The Bluest Eye*. But there are scenes in *The Bluest Eye* that are bits and pieces — my father, he could be very aggressive about people who troubled us — throwing people out and so on, my mother's habit of getting stuck like a record on some problem, going on for days and days and days and then singing in between, you know, just like a saga. You wake up every morning and she has had another chapter of the same problem. (Laughter) And, you know, that curious 30's Depression atmosphere — that was very much there. The rest is fiction. Once the characters are there and they begin to be fully realized and have their own voices, then they really begin to move. They are not at all concerned about facts. And it's less and less true in each successive book. I think most first novels are pretty autobiographical in some way because you are frightened to pull from too many places. Later on I was able to use only the odors or the sounds or the smells of the things I needed. But they are curious places. I knew of a woman named Hannah Peace, for example. I didn't know her well. I just remembered the name and remembered vaguely seeing her, and what I most remembered was the way there was a kind of echo when people called her name. I have no idea of anything about that lady

— nothing really. But I seem to remember that when other people said her name they were saying something else, and I don't know what that was, but I don't really want to know. I just want the taste of it. So that's the kind of thing that's, you know, sort of genuinely autobiographical.

Jones: I am concerned also about your ties with your Alabama past. Is that through your mother exclusively or do you go back yourself? Do you make that pilgrimage at any time?

Morrison: No — I've been back more frequently than she has. She talks about it with affection, but she never goes. My father used to go back to Georgia every year, but although she remembers it with a great deal of pleasure, she never goes there. There is a huge wing of our family who lived in Greenville and then in Birmingham, and that portion of them that didn't come to Ohio went out to California, and I only recently met some of them whom I had only heard stories about. The song in *Song of Solomon* is a song from that wing of the family in Alabama. The song that my mother and aunts know starts out, "Green, the only son of Solomon." And then there are some funny words that I don't understand. It's a long sort of a children's song that I don't remember. But Green was the name of my grandfather's first son and it was a kind of genealogy that they were singing about. So I altered the words for *Song of Solomon*. Those people were born in Greenville.

Jones: At what time in your life did you form specific judgements about the value of being Black?

Morrison: I came to that as a clear statement very late in life, I think, because I left home, say at 17 and went to school, and the things I studied were Western and, you know, I was terrifically fascinated with all of that, and at that time any information that came to me from my own people seemed to me to be backwoodsy and uninformed. You know, they hadn't read all these wonderful books. You know how college students are. And, I think, I didn't regard it as valuable as being Black. I regarded it as valuable as being part of that family because it was an interesting collection of people who had done some rather extraordinary things. I don't mean publicly successful things but, you know, just the way in which they handled crisis situations and life threatening circumstances, so that when I found myself in critical circumstances I literally remembered those people and I thought, "Well, if they could do that, I can do this." It was just that intimate to me. But the consciousness of being Black I think happened when I left Cornell and went to teach at Texas Southern University. You see, I had never been in a Black school like that. I don't mean my awareness was all that intense, but even at Howard University where I went to school, I remember I asked once to do a paper in the English Department on Black Characters in Shakespeare, and they were very much alarmed by that — horrified by it, thought it was a sort of lesser topic, because Howard wasn't really like that. It was very sort of middle class, sort of upwardly mobile and so on. But when I left Cornell and went to Houston, even though I was only there a year and a half, in the South they always had Negro History Week; I'd never heard of it. We didn't have it in the North. (Laughter) But then I began to think about all those books my mother always had in the house — J. A. Rodgers and all those people — and all those incredible conversations my grandfather had and all those arguments that would just hurt my head when I listened to them at the time suddenly had a different meaning. There was a difference between reading the *Call and Post* when it came or the *Pittsburgh Courier* and all the Black papers and then going someplace when there was something called the Black press. So I think it was as a novice teacher, and that was in 1957 or 1958, that I began to think about Black culture as a subject, as an idea, as a discipline. Before it had only been on a very personal level — my family. And I thought they were the way they were because they were my family.

Jones: In what ways did your college teaching experience enhance or deter your creative writing?

Morrison: It deterred it a great deal. (Laughter) I don't think that's the fault of teaching. Some people can teach and write at the same time, write fiction or poetry and do both. I can't do it well; even when I take small jobs it bothers me, only because the mode of thinking is so different. It is analytical. It is taking something apart and examining it, and when I write I am trying to put things together. Also I have to trust something that is ineffable when I write, whereas when I teach I don't trust anything, you know. I try to find out things and I need proof. When I write there is a different side of the brain or a different part of me that's being used, and

| | I find that conflicting. I don't find editing conflicting at all, but I do find teaching because the mode is so different from the mode that I have to be in when I write a novel. So teaching is not helpful to me. |

Jones: What kind of writing schedule do you follow? Do you write everyday.

Morrison: If I'm going well, I do. If I'm not going well, I skip it. I don't write just because I have the time. I write when it's there and then I have to make the time because I find if I have a block of time in order to write and I haven't resolved anything or nothing has come, it's a real waste of time. I just write stuff I have to throw away. So I am a little more compulsive about it, I think, and less disciplined. I operate on compulsion.

Jones: I am fascinated by your effective use of irony as an artistic technique. Would you please comment on why you use irony so profusely?

Morrison: I think that's a Black style. I can't really explain what makes the irony of Black people different from anybody else's, and maybe there isn't any, but in trying to write what I call Black literature which is not merely having Black people in or being Black myself, there seems to be something distinctive about it and I can't put it into critical terms. I can simply recognize it as authentic. Any irony is the mainstay. Other people call it humor. It's not really that. It's not sort of laughing away one's troubles. And laughter itself for Black people has nothing to do with what's funny at all. And taking that which is peripheral, or violent or doomed or something that nobody else can see any value in and making value out of it or having a psychological attitude about duress is part of what made us stay alive and fairly coherent, and irony is a part of that — being able to see the underside of something, as well. I can't think at the moment of any specific instances, but I am conscious of all sorts of things — nature and magic and a kind of mother wit as well as a certain kind of cosmology about how Black people during that time apprehended life simply because they didn't trust anybody else's version of it. That's why I can't trust much research when I do novels because most of the information I want is not written. I mean I can't go to most history books. I can go to some now, I suppose, but certain kinds of things I have to either remember them or be reminded of them or something. It's an area of risk that a writer takes.

Jones: I detect many Greek tragic patterns in your novels, especially in *Song of Solomon*. Do you see any relationship between Greek tragedy and the Black experience?

Morrison: Well, I do. I used to be a little confused about it, and I thought it was just because I was a Classics minor that it was important to me. But there was something about the Greek chorus, for example, that reminds me of what goes on in Black churches and in jazz where there are two things. You have a response obviously. The chorus being the community who participates in this behavior and is shocked by it or horrified by it or they like or they support it. Everybody is in it. And it has something also to do with the way in which those stories are told because the reader becomes a participant in the books, and I have to make it possible for the reader to respond the way I would like the chorus to in addition to the choral effects in the book itself. In the last book I wrote I was deliberately trying to make a choral witness out of the whole world of nature so that butterflies say stuff and, you know, the characters were watched by all that there was. Natural phenomena not only commented on actions, they did so with passion. They had opinions about events but they didn't precipitate any action, yet they were very much involved. And the same sort of participation in churches and even when we were sitting around telling stories, the stories were never the property of the teller. They were community property or they were family property and anybody could elaborate on them or change them or retell them. You heard them over and over again. And there was some quality in them that was stark. There was probably also catharsis in the sense of a combination of the restoration of order — order is restored at the end — and the character having a glimmering of some knowledge that he didn't have when the book began. So everybody complains, well, not everybody, but a lot of people complain about my endings, because it looks like they are falling apart. But something important has happened; some knowledge is there — the Greek knowledge — what is the epiphany in Greek tragedy. But in addition to that, it's community oriented, all of this because the door is open. I don't shut doors at the end of books. There is a resolution of a sort but there are always possibilities — choices, just knowing what those choices are or being able to make a commitment about those choices or knowing something that you would never have known had you not have had that experience — meaning the book. You know, whatever that character knows at the end about herself and her friend could not have happened, whatever Nel knows finally about her relationship with Sula, could not have been clear without the experience of the book. Theirs is a very peculiar relationship. Nel discovered what a friend is — someone you really don't have to explain anything to. And Milkman at the end of *Song of Solomon* being so overwhelmed and so strong and so full of courage and affection that he is ready to die. So it shouldn't matter whether he dies, so long as he is ready and can. And at the end of *Tar Baby* I wanted the choice to be there, where it's possible for him to make a choice and only to hint at the choice that he makes because the deed is done. It can't be undone. And in that sense it is Greek in the sense that the best you can hope for is some realization and that, you know, a certain amount of suffering is not just anxiety. It's also information.

Jones: It's interesting how you are anticipating my next question. My next question is all of your novels have characters who are driven by strong moral forces. Does this have anything to do with your own moral vision? Your religious convictions, maybe?

Morrison: Oh well, I have difficulties with institutions always. But I don't have any doubts — religious doubts, and I find that at the bottom line, striving toward that kind of perfection is more interesting, more compelling. The effort to be good is just more interesting, more demanding. And I don't trust any judgment that I make that does not turn on a moral axis. I can't keep it up all the time, but that is the compelling force. I am prepared to do without if it doesn't sit well. Now, I have a family of people who were highly religious — that was part of their language. Their sources were biblical. They expressed themselves in that fashion. They took it all very, very seriously, so it would be very difficult for me not to. But they combined it with another kind of relationship, to something I think which was outside the Bible. They did not limit themselves to understanding the world *only* through Christian theology. I mean they were quite willing to remember visions, and signs, and premonitions and all of that. But that there was something larger and coherent, and benevolent was always a part of what I was taught and certainly a part of what I believe.

Jones: I consider *Tar Baby* to be a moral allegory. Is this a valid interpretation? Would you want to comment?

Morrison: It has allegorical characteristics in the sense that one watches the characters get in trouble and try to get out, and they do represent certain poles, and certain kinds of thought, and certain kinds of states of being, and they are in conflict with each other, struggling for sovereignty or some sort of primacy. And there are lessons in that sense, in the sense that if you do the following things this will happen. It's true of some of the other books, not the first two so much but certainly *Song of Solomon*. If you believe that property is more important than earth, this is what you are like — you are like Macon Dead. If you believe that earth is more valuable than property, you are like Pilate. If you believe that the revolution means some action, some violent action, and you follow that all the way through, if killing is part of it, this is the logical consequence of it. You can become just a killer, a torpedo, with the best intentions in the world. In *Tar Baby*, if your values are like Jadine's, very contemporary, then you lose something if the past is anathema to you. On the other hand, if you are like Son and you are only concerned about the past, and you can't accommodate yourself to anything contemporary, you lose also. Most satisfactory evolutions of relationships with people have some sort of balance. These people are extremes, making some attempt to accommodate, but they cannot, so that there is some danger in that. I don't know. I may have some attitude about which one is more right than the other, but in a funny sense that book was very unsettling to me because everybody was sort of wrong. (Laughter) Some more wrong than others. And, you know, you sometimes want A to win or B to win and sometimes I didn't like anybody in there some of the time and everybody most of the time. If you say you are somebody's friend as in *Sula*, now what does that mean? What are the lines that you do not step across? And maybe this is the final thing, the final stroke. My efforts is to look at archetypes.

Jones: I would like to move to influences. Who are the novelists who you feel have had the greatest influence on your writing and in what way or ways?

Morrison: I can't think of one novelist that I could say that about. It doesn't mean that I haven't been overwhelmed by lots of writers. I suppose there is one writer, although I've never — it's not even the writing, but Camara Laye wrote a book called the *Radiance of the King* and that had an enormous effect on me. I cannot spot any of that in my writing because I don't know anybody who really writes the way I do and whose style I like that much to incorporate. It's the kind of job that only somebody else could do. I couldn't comment on those influences.

Jones: Your novels are very rhapsodic in style. What is your musical background?

Morrison: None. I mean I can't play any musical instruments and I can't sing, but my mother and my aunts play and sing all the time. They don't read music. My mother sings all the time. So, you know, I heard it all the time.

Jones: Do you write peotry?

Morrison: No, I don't.

Jones: Your explicit imagery often conceals a wealth of implicit ideas. In this sense your novels are quite poetic. Do you consider this a stylistic device?

Morrison: Oh yes, the image, the pictures, for me — it's what holds it. I can't move along in a chapter or part unless I can see the single thing that makes it clear — almost like a painting. As a matter of fact, in regard to your question about influences, I always think I am much more influenced by painters in my writing than by novelists. I can feel direct influences of painters. I can't feel them in novelists that I have read. I think the language of Black people is just so full of metaphor and imagery — the way they talk is very concrete, is bright, and has a lots of color in it; has pictures. It's heavily loaded graphic-graphic. In addition to its sound, it has its sight — those two things. So it certainly has to sound a certain way, but it has to provoke a certain picture, so that if somebody says, "Oh what harm did I ever do you on my knees?" the "on my knees" is not necessary. "What did I ever do but pray for you. What harm have I ever done you on my knees?" The "on my knees" is the picture. She could have been content with just saying "pray for you," but that was not enough. She wants to impress upon him how it looks to be on her knees praying, you see. Or Milkman coming into the town, and I want to say that this is a little country town, but instead of going on for five or six pages I had to see something there that would say that which is a poetic device. So if I have the women walking down the road with nothing in their hands on their way somewhere, then one knows what kind of village that is. You don't do that in the city. You walk around New York without a purse you might get arrested. People'll think you are running from something. Or peacocks, or the birds dying, you know, all of that is palpable — palpable descriptions that not only can I see them and I hope the reader can see them but from what I choose the meaning behind that vision is that nature is askew, or something is coming together, or something terrible is about to happen. You know, whether it's the thing over Sula's eyes which doesn't define her so much as other people because other people have to get themselves together in her presence because she is not helpful in any way; so that they see in her what they wish to see not only in her birthmark but in her because she was wanton, experimental, genuinely dangerous, morally dangerous person.

Jones: Grotesque elements are evident in all of your novels. Why did the grotesque occur to you as an appropriate vehicle for demonstrating the experiences of your characters?

Morrison: Well, I think my goal is to see really and truly of what these people are made, and I put them in situations of great duress and pain, you know, I "call their hand." And, then when I see them in life threatening circumstances or see their hands called, then I know who they are. And some of the situations are grotesque. These are not your normal everyday lives. They are not my normal everyday life, probably not many people's. It's not that I deny that part of life in life. It just doesn't produce anything for me. If I see a person on his way to work everyday doing what he is supposed to do — taking care of his children, then I know that. But what if something really terrible happens, can you still — so that it is always a push towards the abyss somewhere to see what is remarkable, because that's the way I find out what is heroic. That's the way I know why such people survive, who went under, who didn't, what the civilization was, because quiet as it's kept much of our business, our existence here, has been grotesque. It really has. The fact that we are a stable people making an enormous contribution in whatever way to the society is remarkable because all you have to do is scratch the surface, I don't mean us as individuals but us as a race, and there is something quite astonishing there and that's what peaks my curiosity. I do not write books about everyday people. They really are extraordinary whether it's wicked, or stupid or wonderful or what have you. That may go back to the other question about using models from Greek tragedy which seems to me extremely sympathetic to Black culture and in some ways to African culture.

Jones: The legitimacy of the irrational seems to be the reverse of the more rational "norm" in your novels. Would you comment on this?

Morrison: Yes, with a race of people who were perceived as irrational simply because they did not always see the world as white people did, they were regarded as irrational (laughter), but they weren't. You know, their experience simply dictated certain things. They don't seem irrational to me. They seem extreme and maybe excessive. But for most of them, there is a kind of wonderful logic to what they do. And their conclusions may appear to be irrational. If you think of the thought processes that Pilate has, the way she arrived at where she was, with the limited information she had and some good common sense, she got to that place which is a wonderful place to be. She is one of the two or three people that I've written about that I envy. You know, a certain amount of wide-spiritedness and so on. Although I can't recommend that anybody choose that life style, it has got to be based on some legitimate information and a careful analysis without benefit of the traditional kind of education that teaches us what the rational is. That's what distinguishes the colonized from the colonists, viewing what is rational and what is not.

Jones: How important are outrage and anarchy in the attempts of your characters to gain or regain their natural heritage?

Morrison: For some of them, very important. That's the way they do it — like Son. For others its anathema like Macon Dead, and Jadine, and Sydney and Ondine. They don't like that. They are proud people and they take pride in their labor. They like to do things well. They have that sort of elegant way of handling things and they've made their peace with that and they know how to get on in the world step by step, by step, by step, by step. They play with the house cards, and they are not like those people who are not playing with the house deck. They are out to change it, fix it, ignore it, cut off their noses, in many instances to spite their own faces. They're just not going to do it. Many men who are outlaws, not so much contemporary type outlaws but the outlaws that I knew in my youth (laughter), were just those kinds of people. They were, oh, I don't know, episodic; they were adventurers. They felt that they had been dealt a bad hand, and they just made up other rules. They couldn't win with the house deck and that was a part of their daring. So they looked at and that was solution to them, whereas other Black people — they were horrified by all that "bad" behavior. That's all a part of the range of what goes on among us, you know. And until we understand in our own terms what our rites of passage are, what we need in order to nourish ourselves, what happens when we don't get that nourishment, then what looks like erratic

	behavior but isn't will frighten and confuse us. Life becomes comprehensible when we know what rules we are playing by.
Jones:	I am very interested in folklore. My doctoral dissertation was on Black folklore. What are some of your sources for the folklore in your novels?
Morrison:	Almost always something I heard literally, and the way I heard it. The tar baby story varies from some versions, but that's the way I heard it. It was a woman, a girl, with a bonnet (laughter), and flying Africans, not stories, just people saying you know, flying before they came here. It is usually something that I have literally heard. Now, I did check on certain things about people who fly by reading those old slave narratives. It was fascinating because everybody else had heard of that or saw, or knew somebody who saw it. Nobody said, "I never heard of that," you know. "What do you mean flying African?" So it was already there although it was after the fact. I was willing to go ahead with it as a motivating thing for *Song of Solomon*. But the interesting thing about those stories is that I only use the stories I have heard; it gives my work a certain authenticity, but I don't stop there. I try to look underneath it and to see if there is something more because some of that stuff is not only history, it's prophecy. If you look as I do in an imaginative way, you find out all sorts of things that are there that have just been pushed off as children's stories which is absurd. The way people learn — narrative, you know. Myth is the first information there is, and it says realms more than what is usually there. But I don't study

folklore — they are family stories and neighborhood stories and community stories.

Jones: What do you feel is the role of the Black artist in the unfolding development of Black culture?

Morrison: Well, I think — well, I can't speak about the Black artist. I can speak about the Black writer. I suppose all artists have either to bear witness or effect change — improvement — take cataracts off people's eyes in an accessible way. It may be soothing; it may be painful, but that's his job — to enlighten and to strengthen. But as a writer, I think that because things have changed so much and the communities seem to be so much in flux, or, if they are not, they are receiving a deluge of ideas from all parts of the world, it's like being under siege, you know. It takes some effort to keep a family together, a neighborhood together. So since that is the case, the old stories don't work any more and songs don't work any more, that folk art that kept us alive. So now I think novels are important because they are socially responsible. I mean, for me a novel has to be socially responsible as well as very beautiful. If you don't have anything new to say about that which is old or fresh to say, then probably it doesn't need to be written. Fifty years ago, novels were not important for the Black community. I don't mean just reading a good story either. I mean a novel written a certain way can do precisely what spirituals used to do. It can do exactly what blues or jazz or gossip or stories or myths or folklore did — that stuff that was a common well-spring of ideas and again the participation of the reader in it as though it's not alien to him. The people he may not know, but there is some shared history.

Jones: Has the feminist movement influenced your treatment of characters?

Morrison: Not yet. Not yet. I guess Jadine was contemporary or feminist becaust I usually don't write books about now — that was the only book. The other one ended in 1960. This one came up a little closer. It's very difficult to write about a twenty-five year old. They haven't done anything so you can't get anything together. But certainly she would be the recipient of the alertness of the feminine movement now. She would not tolerate, for example, all sorts of things that Son, being a little bit more old-fashioned, rooted, would lay upon her. She was a feminist woman, feminist in that sense. In the long passage in which she is so "I am," "somebody" is thinking about those warrior ants which is her beginning notion of what nurturing ought to be. There is conflict there between what she perceives as woman's probable fate compared to what warrior ants do which are all female which is a life of power, keeping the kingdom going, burying, feeding, you know. It's a tough thing that sort of nourishing, but it's not soft, not girlish. And that is conflicting with what Ondine tells her abut what a woman is. A woman has to be a daughter before she can be any kind of woman. If she doesn't have that in mind, if she doesn't know how to relate to her ancestors, to her tribe, so to speak, she is not good for much. Well, that is directly at odds with her forward looking, futuristic self — "I can't be bound." You know, she wants "freedom." So that's something that I was trying to suggest that she might find out about. At least, she's going back to find out with all her faculties more or less intact.

Jones: I maybe should have asked this question earlier, but to me Pilate is the most singular character in all of your novels. What was your inspiration for creating her?

Morrison: Oh, I don't know. Truth is she sort of looks like a lot of people. But she really sort of appeared full-blown. I mean, I don't think I thought her up. It would be hard to just sit around — and you know, she came that way. She came without a navel. And I just thought that was the most ridiculous thing I had ever heard of. But I kept seeing her that way with that flat stomach. And I put it in perfectly prepared to take it out because it looked funny, but it worked that way. Very early I knew that was the case. It did a couple of things. It made her an outsider in a way and invent herself in a way, which accounted for her eccentricity, but also it made it possible for the whole concept of the combination of that which is real and that which is surreal to work hand in hand because if you can get to that part and accept that, then, you know, anything might happen which is what does happen. In order to make the reader swallow the flying African, which is what one has to do, at least metaphorically, if not actually. I was trying to think what really would it take to fly. Let's think about it as a real thing. Then having this aberration appear early, it not only worked for her character but for the whole theme of the book. So I had to — I was very happy to use it. Starting from what is an unsullied development, she has a combination of the wonder of childhood and is very sage about other things. She is very sweet and nurturing and also very fierce. And she really does combine for me, and I think that is what makes her unique, some male and female characteristics blended well so they work as opposed to Sula who did what men do which is what made her so terrible. I mean she behaves so terribly. (Laughter) It was so terrrible because it was askew. It was awful. She didn't care anything about anybody. But Pilate is a loving, caring woman, nevertheless. And she is so clear about herself. She has total respose and total trust of her own instincts. And once I found the way that she could become and stay in this world, then she was unlike everybody. Eva was sort of like that, but she was very managerial, she named people and controlled people. She didn't like for anybody to buck her either. This woman Pilate is not interested in possession. She has no vanity.

Jones: You've been a dancer, an actress, a teacher, an editor, and now a novelist. What's next for Toni Morrison? Are you going to continue your writing? When can we expect another novel? I want to be the first to hear it.

Morrison: (Laughter) Yes, I have a sort of novel that's humming in my earlobes and it has not pattern yet. It's just an idea that I want to develop. I am not ready to commit myself to four years of hardship right now. (Laughter) So I am trying to let it arrive. I am not going to go looking for it. But I can tell when something is sort of up in there.

Jones: Is economics the overriding issue in the lives of Black Americans?

Morrison: Well, I wish it were that simple. It seems as though it is, but it is something more sinister than that. Poverty is not good for you, but it doesn't have to be depraved. There is something disjointed — now mind you when I say this I am very much influenced by living in New York city — but it's like somebody skipped a beat. It's like you used to be born Black, and that meant something. It meant when you saw another Black person you knew all sorts of things right away. And no matter what kind of financial situation they were in, you know, you all went to the same hairdresser and all went to the same beauty parlor. There were some things you could count on, some language, some shared assumptions. That doesn't seem to be true now. Being Black now is something you have to choose to be. Choose it, no matter what your skin color. I used to always feel safe among Black people. I did. I don't anymore, just because they are Black. And that for me is a huge jump. I'm in betwixt this generation of people who could go into any Black neighborhood and be safe. (Laughter) Somebody told me that their grandmother said that she had come to Philadelphia sixty years ago. And she said, "When I saw a Black man, I thought, 'I am safe. Thank God.' But now when I see a Black man, I think I ought to run." Something has happened. You see we are very close now to the society that is around us. I don't mean that the structures that held us together are gone, but there are new things pressing in our lives — new modes, new music, new menus, television, you know, and it's like going to the city. Stevie Wonder has a little song (laughter) "Living Just for the City." It's not enough. So I am a little bit alarmed by the changes. Maybe I shouldn't be. Maybe I should move. (Laughter) You know there are still lovely places. But I even see it in Lorain, Ohio. Just — I keeping thinking — the children are really in danger — our children.

Jones: What is your view regarding the future of the American family?

Morrison: Well, there seems to be some awareness now of its value as a little microcosm. There was a time when everybody left home to go do it — succeed. And parents encouraged that — going out in order to make it. And parents wanted their children to do better then they did. The bad part of that is that they do like Jadine. They just do better and they forget these people. Now, it might be sort of strife-ridden. Now, there seems to be some form of reclamation that's going on with the family's reclaiming itself. Part of that has to do, I think, with the knowledge that it's under stress. Part of it is economics. You know, young married couples always used to live some place else. Now, you know, children are coming home and staying home. It's not that little nuclear family — everybody striving for that nuclear family way off somewhere, you know. The times are so scary. It's so frightening that people are grouping back together. But I see it even in the people who are away from home. They make up substitute families. You know, work families, commune families or avocation families. Even if you are not with your family you make up another group of people that serve or function almost as your family. So I am optimistic about that, because your family is like a little, tiny world. Most people's families represent practically everything that you can find — out there. So if you can't get along with them you might as well forget it (laughter) because they are all out there in the street. You know, all the wonderful ones, the terrible ones, the lunatics, the sane, the nicies. Go to any family reunion, and there it is. All the old enmities, the old friendships, all that's right there. If you run away from it, you find it duplicated in other situations. You just take the harm out of it.

Jones: Well, the final inevitable question. Ms. Morrison, what advice would you give to the young Black novelists in the eighties?

Morrison: Well — they are in a pretty good position for writing now because there are a lot of good Black writers around, and twenty years ago there were fewer. So they have a lot of good things to read, and that is the only advice I have for any writer is to read. It's like any other craft. You have to know the industry and know what has been done. And then when you read and find something you like, try to figure out why you like it, what they did, and that's how you develop your draft. Not imitation, not even emulation, but just this wide range of reading. And then have that combination of respect for the language and contempt, so you can break it. But you have to know what it is before you can break it. You can't break any rule that you don't know. This is the language that we speak, and one should know all there is to know about it. Everything.

QUESTIONS

1. To what extent did Miss Morrison use her own hometown and family background in her novels?

2. In Miss Morrison's opinion, how is irony related to a Black style?

3. To what extent does Miss Morrison use imagery as a stylistic device in her novels?

4. For what purpose does Miss Morrison state that she uses the grotesque in her novels?

5. Point out some of Miss Morrison's source of folklore.

6. Describe Miss Morrison's conception of Pilate Dead.

7. What is Miss Morrison's view regarding the future of the American family?

8. Give a succinct statement of Miss Morrison's advice to the young black novelist.

BIBLIOGRAPHY

Bodkin, Maud. *Archetypal Patterns*. New York: Vantage Books, 1958.

Brooks, Cleanth, R. W. Lewis and Robert Penn Warren, eds. *American Literature: The Makers and the Making*. New York: St. Martin's Press, 1973.

Campbell, Joseph. *The Hero with a Thousand Faces*. Cleveland: World Publishing Company, 1956.

Morrison, Toni. *The Bluest Eye*. New York: Holt, Rinehart and Winston, 1970.

_____. *Song of Solomon*. New York: Alfred A. Knopf, Inc., 1977.

_____. *Sula*. New York: Alfred A. Knopf, Inc., 1973.

_____. *Tar Baby*. New York: Alfred A. Knopf, Inc., 1981.

INDEX

Ajax, 14
Anderson, Sherwood, 7
"At a Solemn Music," 120

Bluest Eye, The, 1, 8,
  15, 25, 93
Bodkin, Maud, 40, 42
Bottom, 12, 18, 39, 50,
  51, 59
Brecht, Bertolt, 20
Brooks, Cleanth, 37
Byron, Lord, 44

Campbell, Joseph, 73
Chicken Little, 18
Circe, 68, 75, 76, 91,
  99
Cholly, 28, 29, 30, 90
Church, Soaphead, 13, 33
Claudia, 17, 20, 26-27,
  31, 41

Dante, 18
Dead, Macon I, 41, 89,
  104
Dead, Macon II, 41, 65,
  69, 104
Dead, Macon III
  (Milkman), 3, 43, 72, 74,
  84, 97, 105, 109
Dead, Ruth, 11, 104,
  106, 107
Deweys, The, 14, 52, 53

Eloe, 45

Faulkner, William, 7,
  21, 63, 98

Ferlinghetti, Lawrence, 9
First Corinthians, 11, 12
Frieda, 23, 26-27, 31,
  41

Gaines, Ernest J., 9
Gorky, Maxim, 50
Guitar, 3, 21, 73, 89,
  90, 92, 96, 98
Hagar, 15, 68, 108
Hannah, 18, 57, 108, 129
Hero with a Thousand Faces, 73

Isle de Chevaliers, 19, 44,
  115ff

Jadine, 4, 5, 21, 44, 45
Jones, Bessie, W., 19

Laye, Camara, 139
Lorain, 127
Lytle, Andrew, 7

Magdalena, 14
Medallion, 50, 57, 59
Mercy Hospital, 63
Meta-realism, 7
Milkman, 3, 10, 43, 65, 72,
  74, 84, 97
Milton, John, 115-116

Nell, 2, 43, 58

O'Connor, Flannery, 7

Paradise Lost, 115-116
Pauline, 8, 28ff, 37-38
Peace, Eva, 6, 9, 14, 16, 52,
  54, 55

Pecola, 1, 20, 21, 27ff, 38
Peal, Maureen, 8-9, 27
Pilate, 11, 63, 65ff, 81, 110, 147
Plum, 7, 16, 18
Pretty, Johnny, 14

Radiance of the King, 139
Seven Days, The, 94, 95, 97
Shadrack, 14, 16, 18, 51, 52, 93
Shakespeare, William, 30, 81
Shalimar, 85, 103
Smith, Robert, 12, 64
Solomon, 103
Son, 19, 45, 46, 121
Song of Solomon, 2, 12, 21, 41, 89, 103, 144
Street, Margaret, 12, 117
Street, Valerian, 117, 119
Sula, 18, 21, 56, 57, 58
Sula, 12, 16, 17, 39, 43, 49, 93
Tar Baby, 53-54
Tar Baby, 4, 18, 21, 44, 115ff
Tempest, The, 81
Temple, Shirley, 20
Therese, 12, 15
Till, Emmett, 95
Velvet Horn, 7
Vinson, Audrey, L., 127
Welty, Eudora, 7
Wonder, Stevie, 150
Wordsworth, William, 119
Wright, Richard, 7